GW00367289

TEN ADVENTUROUS

WALKS IN

HAMPSHIRE

Raymond Hugh

Illustrations by
Jackie Hei

ISBN 1 874476 02 0

Published by Morning Mist Publishing 1993
P.O. Box 108, Reigate, Surrey RH2 9YP.
© Raymond Hugh and Jackie Hei 1993

Designed and Printed by
Advanced Data Graphics, Sevenoaks

INDEX

INTRODUCTION

THE ADVENTURE

The adventure must be yours, it is the thrill of exploration, the pleasure of experiencing something new and the surprise of the unexpected. You could do the same walk several times and each time it will be different. On a summer's day you can watch trout sunning in crystal waters. In winter a heron risking the lashing rain to find a meal when the waters are murky. On a crisp frosty morning, it can seem that the whole of Hampshire is visible. On another, you may be lucky to find your next step!The weather not only changes the appearance of a walk, it can also change the feel. The adventure is discovering the secrets of the route on the day.

THE REWARD

The reward is the sense of achievement and the knowledge that not only have you completed a respectable distance, you will have learned and experienced something of Hampshire which before was a mystery. There is no greater satisfaction than to discover the county as our ancestors did, on foot.

WHEN TO GO

Many walkers make the mistake of only walking in fine weather, leaving the hills at the slightest sign of rain. In wet and windy weather the countryside is untamed and with the majority of the population safe in their houses, one can really get a feeling of remoteness and a better idea of what Hampshire was like several hundred years ago. My suggestion is that you try and do the walks in all seasons and all weathers. At the end if you don't hate me, you will really begin to feel an affinity with the Hampshire countryside and the satisfaction of knowing the county well. As for the time of day, I recommend that you try and time your walk to include either dawn or dusk. These to me are the best part of the day, unfortunately often missed by the majority.

PREPARATION

Planning the walk is as important and as enjoyable as doing the walk itself. Firstly consider whether you want to make a weekend of it. If you do, then I suggest that you book local accommodation. This not only cuts down on travelling on the day, but creates a seemingly longer weekend and allows you to remain familiar with the area at night.

There is nothing better in my mind than to finish a long walk and retire to local accommodation for a hot bath before a well earned visit to the local village pub, without having to worry about driving home. A selection of recommended accommodation is listed at the end of each walk.

Once you have decided on your walk, familiarise yourself with it. Read the walk through, following it on the map, to ensure you understand where it is you are going. The route descriptions contain points of interest and you may want to take time to stop and visit these. If you do, it might be worth borrowing a book from the Library to read up before your visit. When you have made up your mind on the points of interest to visit, try and estimate the length of your walk. The timings given on each walk are meant as a rough guide only and are based on a person being reasonably fit. If you are unsure, then I suggest you allow for approximately two miles per hour. Timing is important as you could find yourself stumbling back to the start in the dark.

Finally, make sure you are fit. The walks in this book are longer than the average walking book and can be hard work if you are unprepared. To help identify the gradients, a cross section is included at the start of each walk.

WHAT TO TAKE

A good map is essential. I recommend you use the Ordnance Survey Landranger maps and the start of each walk details the map(s) required. You can also use the Ordnance Survey Pathfinder maps which have far more detail such as field boundaries, but they can be harder to find and can ultimately be more expensive.

Once armed with your map, make sure you have sensible clothing. This means clothes which are loose and comfortable. Tight jeans and high heels are not recommended! No matter how good the weather is at the start of the day, always pack some waterproofs. Being caught out in the rain without the necessary protection is not an experience I would recommend. In summer if you are walking in shorts, waterproof trousers are also particularly useful as a temporary protection against nettles. There is a wide range of waterproof clothing now available. The two recommendations I would make are:-

(1) Make sure you are completely covered, that is buy trousers and a jacket.

(2) Buy clothing made from one of the breathable materials - your local stockist will advise you on these.

If the weather is cold, then gloves and a hat are always advisable. No matter what time of year, I always pack a jumper and have never regretted it. Keeping warm helps avoid tiredness. Most importantly, make sure you have a good pair of shoes. If you can afford it, then buy a pair of walking boots. If not, then make sure your shoes are strong, comfortable and have soles with a good grip. Equally important are good socks. If you have boots then two pairs are advisable. Do not think that the socks you wear in the office will do!

Sensibly clothed, you can now think about other equipment you may need. A camera and a pair of binoculars are always useful and can enhance your day out. I always carry a pocket book on birds, you could do the same or add to this with a book on local flora or history. You will find the the walk all the more enjoyable for a little bit of knowledge. Do not, though, get over enthusiastic and take a library or you may find yourself requiring a book on first aid!

A basic first aid kit though is always advisable. The Hampshire countryside may appear tame and so it is, compared to the Himalayas, but must still be treated with respect. The book and the map should be enough to find the route without difficulty, however a compass is always useful for finding your way when paths are undefined.

Refreshments are always an important consideration. There are places where you can get a bite to eat on every walk but even if you wish to use their facilities it is important to carry some basic snacks, especially in cold weather. You should always carry water and a thermos flask with hot soup or drink can also be very welcome. To carry all this one should have a comfortable day sack or small rucksack. These are now available from a wide assortment of shops, but before you purchase one, make sure it's strong and more importantly ensure it's comfortable.

Finally take your five senses with you - these are essential if you are to fully appreciate the walk and most importantly, **ENSURE YOU TAKE THIS BOOK!**

GETTING THERE

Most people will be mobile, i.e. a car or bicycle. Where practical I have listed railway stations, however buses are far more difficult as their routes and timetables tend to change with the wind. For those people relying on a bus to reach the start, I have listed the main bus companies serving the area below:-

Alder Valley (Tel: 0420 83787)

Coastline Express (Tel: 0705 498894)

County Bus (Tel: 0962 868944)

Hampshire Bus (Tel: 0962 852352)

Hants & Sussex (Tel: 0243 372045)

Meon Valley Community Bus (Tel: 0489 877714)

Solent Blue Line (Tel: 0703 226235)

Hampshire County Council publish an excellent public transport map which details most of the bus routes throughout the county. The map can be obtained from local Tourist and Information centres or by phoning: 0962 868944.

ROUTE FINDING

The route descriptions are instructional rather than poetic and should be followed without difficulty. To assist you a series of symbols in the left hand margin enable you to identify specific points on the walk at a glance. A good map is essential and should be used in conjunction with the route description. Please remember that like everything else, the countryside changes with time, a fenced path can become unfenced and vice versa.

Before setting out, make sure you have identified the route on the map. To pinpoint a starting point or place of interest and key points on the route, I have used grid references which are printed in bold in the text. These are six figured numbers which identify a particular point on the map. Every Ordnance Survey map is covered by a national grid. The grid's lines are identified by numbers printed on the map's surround. To find a grid reference, take the first three numbers which refer to the vertical lines on your map and locate them on the top or bottom (north or south) of the map. The third number is an imaginary line in the square following the first two numbers. To find this line, divide the square into ten equal parts. Then take the latter three numbers, which refer to the horizontal lines and locate them on the left or right (east or west) of your map and follow the line of this reference until it meets the line of the first reference. Their meeting point is the grid reference point itself. Do not rely on the maps in this book, these are not to scale and are meant as a rough guide only.

It is important that you recognise the various types of footpath signs. Most are fairly obvious, i.e. wooden post with a sign marked "footpath" or "public bridleway", pointing in the direction of the right of way. Some will have the name of a specific route, for example, "Wayfarers Walk".

Over recent years many County Councils have standardised their signs to follow national guidelines. Footpaths are now shown with a yellow arrow and bridleways with a blue one. Like the old wooden signs the arrows will point in the direction of the right of way. Some arrows will have the initials of a recognised walk imprinted, though this is still rare in Hampshire. On top of all this, you will often find custom built signs. These can mark an official route but more often than not, are the work of local farmers guiding the walker across their land. An example of the former is Avon Valley Path which is highlighted by a green arrow bearing a bridge symbol on a beige background.

An important rule on route finding is to take your time, follow the map and read the route description thoroughly. If you do this then you will return to base without mishap.

LONG DISTANCE WALKS

Many of the routes meet long distance linear walks which run through Hampshire. In case you want to try any I have listed their names, with distances, below, along with the publisher who produces a description of the walk.

Avon Valley Path - 34 miles (Hampshire County Council - leaflet)

Clarendon Way - 24 miles (Hampshire County Council)

Hanger Way - 17 miles (Hampshire County Council - leaflet)

Itchen Way - 27 miles (Countryside Books)

King Alfreds Way - 108 miles (Thornhill Press)
King John Way - 60 miles (Pat Hayers)
Pilgrims Way - 116 miles (Constable)
Severn to Solent Walk - 120 miles (Thornhill Press)
Solent Way - 60 miles (Hampshire County Council)
South Downs Way (extension) - 28 miles (Eastbourne Rambling Club)
South Wessex Way - 117 miles (Thornhill Press)
Test Way - 44 miles (Hampshire County Council)
Wayfarers Walk - 70 miles (Hampshire County Council)

AUTHOR'S NOTE

Every effort has been made to ensure that the route descriptions are accurate. Time changes things however and can alter the description of the route. If you have any difficulty in finding any part of a route, please write with details, giving a grid reference, to enable me to re-examine the route. A free copy of the next publication will be forwarded for any suggestions used in the next edition. Enjoy your walks.

THE HIGH HAMPSHIRE HOBBLE

Distance: 10 1/2 miles (17 km)

Time: Allow approximately 5 hours

Map: Ordnance Survey Landranger Map 174

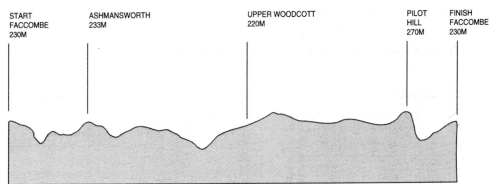

START	ASHMANSWORTH	UPPER WOODCOTT	PILOT	FINISH
FACCOMBE	233M	220M	HILL	FACCOMBE
230M			270M	230M

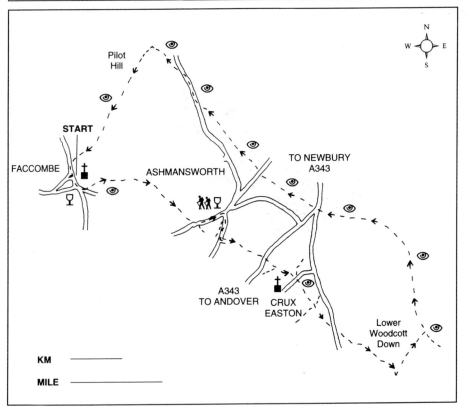

1

Walk Summary

This walk in the north west corner of Hampshire, explores the beautiful north Hampshire downs. The walk title is most appropriate as on the route you discover the highest hill, the highest village, the highest pub and even the highest sewage treatment plant in Hampshire! Surprisingly you might think, there are few steep ascents with much of the walk being along a ridge. Apart from the hills, the walk passes through a couple of pretty villages, both with inviting hostelries. One word of warning, in winter the walk is not for the faint hearted, much of the route becomes very muddy and the northerly winds hit the downs with a biting ferocity which can sap even the most dedicated explorer's enthusiasm.

Start - OS. 390581 Map 174

The walk starts from the church at Faccombe. The easiest way to get there is to take the A343 between Newbury and Andover. If coming from Newbury, stay on the road until you reach the ridge of the downs where just after passing Three Legged Cross, a house on the left, take a turning right signposted to Ashmansworth. On reaching Ashmansworth, turn left in front of The Plough and after a few metres, turn right onto a lane signposted to Faccombe. Follow the lane to its end where you turn right into the village of Faccombe. If coming from Andover, stay on the A343 and just after passing through Hurstbourne Tarrant, take a turning left opposite a garage signposted to Netherton, Faccombe and Linkenholt. Follow the lane for approximately one mile and then take a turning right signposted to Faccombe and Ashmansworth. Stay on the lane to reach Faccombe village. A good alternative start is the village of Ashmansworth. Starting here means you can make the inn at Faccombe your lunch time stop. Parking in both villages is limited so please be considerate. The nearest railway station is at Newbury.

THE HIGH HAMPSHIRE HOBBLE

Before starting proper, it is worth knowing something of Faccombe village.

Faccombe (OS. 390581 Map 174) is just three metres short of being the highest village in Hampshire. Looking around, you soon realise a similarity in many of the houses. This is because almost the entire village is owned by Faccombe Estates as is much of the surrounding countryside. Apart from some pretty cottages, Faccombe boasts a superb manor house, a typical village pond with a pleasant shelter from where you can observe the ducks without getting wet and opposite the pond a cosy village inn, The Jack Russell. The church which stands at the centre of the village is relatively modern, though a few artefacts from the original church still remain, including the font which is over eight hundred years old.

For refreshments, The Jack Russell, a free house, offers a good selection of ale and if this doesn't warm you up, it also serves some excellent food.

From the village church, start walking south through the village passing to the right of the manor house. Ignore a turning off to the right to "The Jack Russell" pub and shortly after, take a turning left signposted to Ashmansworth and Highclere, to follow a brick and flint wall on the left.

Just after the wall ends take the first signposted footpath left and go over a stile into a field. Go straight across the field in the direction of the footpath sign, to reach and cross another stile at the far side.

After the stile carry straight on going over a crossing track and follow a grass track gently downhill. The track soon enters woodland where you should ignore a track off to the left. A few paces on however, you should take the next turning left to leave the woodland and follow a track steeply downhill.

On reaching a farm track near the valley bottom, turn right along the track to continue your route downhill. At the bottom of the valley proper, go straight across a crossing track to follow a track ahead, signposted as a footpath. The two flint buildings on your right here are all that remains of "Curzon Farm". This is one of several farms in the area which disappeared in recent years. This is despite the rich soil which prompted a farmer from another deserted farm in the same valley, to boast that he could pick small fruit from his garden on Christmas Day. The rich soil still exists and is probably the very reason why bigger enterprises bought out these smaller farms.

The track takes you between fields and up the other side of the valley with views to your left as you progress of Pilot Hill, the highest hill in Hampshire and Combe Hill with its two prominent aerial masts. On nearing the top of the hill, ignore a track off to the right to enter woodland. Almost immediately after, the track forks and you should take the right hand fork, still signposted as a footpath, to follow the track through the wood. The track soon leads you out of the wood where shortly after you should go over a crossing track to continue ahead through a newly established plantation. It then runs through the centre of the plantation and your way, at the time of writing, is guided by white arrows.

You will soon reach a field with excellent views to your right across a wide valley. Again, at the time of writing, a temporary stile links your route into the field. From here, you should go straight across the centre of the field where, as a guide, the wood on your left is Privet Copse. Approximately half way across the field, do not make the mistake of heading for a farm track leading ahead, but bear towards the left hand corner of the field and another temporary stile. Go over the stile which takes you onto a farm track.

Cross the farm track and take a narrow marked footpath through a gap in the hedge ahead. The footpath takes you downhill through a small copse to meet another track. Go over the farm track and carry straight on across the centre of a field ahead in the direction of the footpath sign. After a short distance, the footpath follows the right hand perimeter of another copse and then meets another field. You should go straight across the field bearing gently left heading for a farm gate and stile the other side. Go over the stile to reach a narrow lane.

War memorial Ashmansworth

Turn left along the lane and follow this uphill into the village of Ashmansworth. Shortly after joining the lane, you will spot a footpath on your right. If you do not wish to visit Ashmansworth, you can take this to reach another lane where you should turn left for a few metres to then rejoin our route by taking a track right, marked as a footpath (**OS. 414570**). Our route proper however, is uphill along the lane to arrive at Ashmansworth, ignoring another footpath off to the right as we do so.

Ashmansworth (OS. 416575 Map 174) *is the highest village in Hampshire and boasts an excellent free house, The Plough, the highest pub in Hampshire. It seems a shame* *don't you think, not to rest a while and enjoy the highest pint in Hampshire! At the southern end of the village (where we enter) is a small green with a war memorial. The village church is a mile further south attached to the appropriately named Church Farm.*

To continue our route, on entering the village turn right in front of the village green and right again to walk away from the village centre along a lane which runs between houses. You will soon pass a sewage treatment plant on the left, the highest plant in Hampshire! Soon after, you will meet a farm on your right where you should look out for an old track on the left, marked as a footpath. This is also the point at which the short cut mentioned earlier, rejoins our route **(OS. 414570)**.

Take the farm track known locally as Hipple Lane, downhill taking care especially in wet weather when the track doubles as a stream and therefore, can be extremely wet and muddy. The track runs between banks and soon meets a field where you should stay on the track following the right hand perimeter of the field, still going downhill. On your right, as a guide, is a steep ditch, once the line of the original track and now overgrown. Soon after, the track leads out of the fields to run through scrubland and then winds on to take you through a copse eventually meeting a field.

Just before the field, look out for a stile on the left which you should cross to take a narrow footpath downhill along the edge of the copse. You will soon meet another stile which you should cross into a field. Go straight over a crossing track and continue ahead, now going uphill along the right hand perimeter of the field. As the field perimeter gives way on your right, you should continue your course ahead across the field to go over the crest of the hill. Once over the hill, you should head for a stile at the far side.

Go over the stile and go straight across the centre of the next field, heading for a farm gate and the main road, the A343. Cross the road and enter a field the other side and go straight across the field in the direction of the footpath sign, heading for another farm gate at the far side. Pass through the gate and take a track ahead going gently uphill, to soon pass two cottages on the left. These are still known as "The Faithfuls", the name of the family that first lived in them. Stay on the track which later skirts around a pond heading for the hamlet of Crux Easton. You should ignore a footpath and stile off to the left and continue to meet a lane which runs through the heart of the hamlet.

***Crux Easton (OS. 427564 Map 174)** is somewhat humble in appearance with no grand buildings to state its presence and yet if you look more closely this unassuming hamlet hides a rich and varied past. Indeed, the hamlet has a number of monuments which make it stand out from other similar hamlets in Hampshire. The first to your right on a small green behind a post and phone box, is a tree. Look more closely and you will see a small stone memorial at its foot. The inscription reads "Planted in 1894 in memory of the church restoration by Mrs. Wake of Church Easton Farm". A nice and rare touch by someone who took pride in their surroundings.*

A scene from Crux Easton

The church to which the memorial refers is a small brick Georgian affair at the end of the lane to your right. Like the hamlet it serves, it is a humble affair but it too has a past worth revealing. From the church are a number of tunnels leading to the manor house, the old rectory and school. Unfortunately, the age and purpose of these tunnels are unknown. One of the vicars of the church was a Reverend Charles de Havilland. It was his son Geoffrey who became the famous aircraft designer and was a pioneer of the aircraft industry in this country. He would often visit his father, arriving in one of his planes at a nearby field. As you can imagine, in its day, this was quite a spectacle.

Crux Easton boasts two more famous inhabitants, the first was Edward Lisle who owned the manor. In 1757 after his death, his son published his still respected book on agriculture, "Observations in Husbandry". One wonders where he got the time, as apart from writing and running the manor, he also managed to father twenty children. The second was Sir Oswald Mosley. He was the founder of the British Union of Fascists and was held at Crux Easton for the duration of the Second World War.

Probably the most distinctive building in the village is the tall wind pump designed to pump water to the manor house. It is the only remaining pump of its kind in the south east of England.

From the tree with its memorial, go straight across the lane to join a tarmac track ahead, passing an old barn and the old wind pump in a field on your right. On your left are a number of houses, the last being a white cottage where the track bends left. Here you should leave the track to continue straight on along a farm track which runs between fields. After a short distance, the track follows a line of trees on your left and now runs along the left hand perimeter of a field.

At the corner of the field the track bends right and you should leave it here to continue straight on, where ahead of you now are two fields divided by a narrow strip of woodland. You should enter the right hand field and then turn left to follow the left hand field perimeter, following the tree line which was directly ahead of you. As you progress, you will continue to enjoy excellent views across Hampshire to your right.

At the far corner of the field, pass through a gap in the hedge in front of you and continue for a few paces before turning left to reach the top corner of another field. From here, you should head diagonally right across the field, heading for a gap in the hedgerow and a footpath sign in the distance. In summer when the crops are high this may at first be difficult to find. You should therefore, walk along the top of the field until the path comes into view. As you cross the field to your right you will see a farm. This is "Upper Woodcott Farm" and beside it is Woodcott church which has a yew tree reputed to be the largest in Hampshire.

At the other side of the field, cross a lane to join a track opposite also signposted as a footpath. The track runs across a field to meet the edge of Hook Copse and then bends right to follow the copse perimeter going gently downhill. Follow the track until it enters a field on your left. Here you should leave it to carry straight on along a footpath which runs through a narrow strip of woodland. This may in summer be slightly hidden, so take care not to miss it. The strip of woodland through which you are now walking acts as a field boundary as well as a footpath and in summer the going may be difficult as the path can be somewhat overgrown.

The footpath descends and passes to the left of some ruins of another deserted farm,

"Hook Farm" and soon after meets a track. You should ignore the track and carry straight on along a narrow footpath which, for a short distance, runs through undergrowth and thereafter, between fields. The footpath eventually ends at a track beside some large barns. Turn right along the track passing the barns on your left and continue to reach a thatched house, "Lower Woodcott Farm" and a lane. Just before the latter, you should leave the track and turn left on to another track which runs uphill behind the barns. This is signposted as a bridleway and takes you over Lower Woodcott Down.

After approximately half a mile, you will reach the northern slopes of Lower Woodcott Down where the track bends right. You should leave the track at this point and turn left through a metal gate bordered by white topped posts, indicating that you are now joining the Wayfarers Walk. A small painted sign, a black arrow on a white background, confirms this. From the hill side you now gain fantastic views across to Beacon Hill opposite, an iron age hill fort and further off to your right, Ladle Hill, another hill fort and beyond that, Watership Down of rabbit fame. The two forts were built to defend the major trade route between the ports on the south coast to the Midlands, now the A34. At the foot of Watership Down made famous by Richard Adams, lives our most famous composer, Andrew Lloyd Webber. If you have time after the walk, then visit his local pub in Ecchinswell, which in my opinion serves the best ale in Hampshire.

You will now follow a grass track through a field which soon forks. Take the left hand fork which follows the left hand field perimeter uphill to go over Upper Woodcott Down. The smart set of stables in the valley below are part of "Highclere Stud Farm", which in turn is part of the Highclere Estate. The stud farm was started in 1902 by the fifth Earl of Carnarvon (famous for discovering along with Howard Carter, the tomb of Tutankhamun) and is now one of the most respected stud farms in the country. The seventh Earl of Carnarvon, in 1969, became the racing manager to the Queen.

After passing a line of conifers on your left, the track descends to meet a metal gate through which you should pass to continue ahead along a now more prominent track. Shortly after, you should ignore a track off to the left and carry straight on, again going uphill. At the top, the track passes through a small picturesque beech wood at which point you will be 266 metres above sea level, the second highest point on the walk with the highest yet to come! You should continue straight on still following the signs for the Wayfarers Walk and ignore a track off to the right leading into the wood. Soon after, the track begins a gradual and pleasant descent to meet and pass another area of woodland on the left which is known as Grotto Copse. There once really was a grotto in this copse, built by nine of the daughters of Edward Lisle of Crux Easton. Sadly, the grotto has disappeared.

Staying on the track, you will soon pass what appears to be another folly. This is a flint and stone building that looks like a miniature castle. It is in fact, a gate house to the Highclere Estate.

Highclere Castle (OS. 446587 Map 174), though not on the route, is worth a mention and perhaps a visit after your walk. The castle is in reality, a house the largest mansion in Hampshire. It is the seat of the Earl of Carnarvon. Surrounding the house is a superb park landscaped by Capability Brown. Probably the house's most famous owner was the fifth Earl of Carnarvon whose

Amun

6

efforts helped find the lost tomb of Tutankhamun and many other treasures of ancient Egypt. Many of these treasures he smuggled out and hid at Highclere. Some have only recently been rediscovered and now form part of an Egyptian exhibition at the house. The house is open through July, August and September, Wednesdays to Sundays.

Follow the track past the gatehouse ignoring a turning off to the left and thereafter another off to the right, to continue ahead. The track, partly tarmacced in places, now runs between fields and occasionally on your right affords views over the Kennet valley in Berkshire. Behind to your right is "Highclere Castle" itself. Follow the track to arrive at a cottage and a narrow lane. Cross the lane and pass to the right of a fairly large house, "The Three Legged Cross", once a pub, to meet the main road, the A343.

Turn left along the main road for approximately twenty paces, where you should cross it to join a track the other side still signposted as the Wayfarers Walk. The track which can be extremely muddy in wet weather, runs along the top of the hill with excellent views to your right of the Kennet valley, Newbury and the Berkshire Downs. The track you are following and in fact since you first joined the Wayfarers Walk, was an ancient neolithic trading route known as The Northants Ridgeway. The route is older than just about any other track in Hampshire and linked a series of forts from Wiltshire to Surrey. As you squelch through the mud, you are literally walking through history.

Follow the track to eventually meet another lane beside a picturesque cottage on the right. Cross the lane to continue along a track the other side, still part of the Wayfarers Walk and signposted as a right of way. The track continues along the ridge for approximately one mile to meet another lane. Turn right along the lane which if you are walking in wet muddy weather, offers some relief underfoot, it also almost immediately offers yet more views right with "Highclere Castle" in the distance and beyond it, Watership Down.

You will soon pass an old brick chimney on the right, the building it served having long since fallen around it. After approximately a quarter of a mile, take a track on the left again signposted as the Wayfarers Walk **(OS. 407598).** The track climbs gently uphill and shortly meets a small copse hiding a house on the left. It then bends left and then right continuing to follow the ridge. From here, you gain perhaps the best views on the walk. You will soon meet a stepped stile on the right where you should turn left to go away from the stile directly across a field. You are now leaving the Wayfarers Walk and should follow the yellow arrows indicating your route is a public footpath. The footpath takes you over Pilot Hill, the highest hill in Hampshire and the highest part of our walk.

At the far side of the field, pass over a low wooden fence and continue ahead through a small copse to reach another field. On meeting the field itself, bear left to follow the edge of the copse round and just as the copse begins to bend away almost back on itself, turn right and go straight across the field along a fairly prominent footpath. As a guide, you should be roughly one hundred metres from the tree line on your left. At the far side, cross a stile into another field where there are spectacular views across a valley to the village of Faccombe on the hill top ahead.

From the stile you should bear diagonally left down the side of the hill to arrive at a prominent track beside a footpath sign. Turn right along the track and follow this steeply downhill where after a short distance, you should ignore a track off to the right before passing through a small metal gate. Continue ahead to pass through a small copse and follow the track to the valley bottom. To your right in the distance are two prominent aerial masts on the top of Combe Hill.

Stay on the track and leave the valley bottom to climb uphill to Faccombe, ignoring any turnings off. This is the last test on your tired legs. Take heart however - if you have timed your walk right you may feel that just reward is waiting for you by way of a refreshing finish at "The Jack Russell" pub. At the top of the hill, you should ignore a track joining from the right and almost immediately after, another coming in from the left to carry straight on.

The track leads out to some houses beside a small green. Turn right along the lane with the green on your left to meet another lane onto which you should turn left and pass the Estate Office on the right. This manages much of the land through which you have been walking today. Follow the lane to arrive at the church, our starting point - or continue for a few paces more for that well earned drink at "The Jack Russell"!

ACCOMMODATION

Esseborne Manor, Hurstbourne Tarrant. Tel: 026476 444

One and three quarter miles from the walk, this is a very personal hotel offering quality but discreet comfort. The comfort does come at a price but after a hard day's walking you deserve it.

The Jack Russell, Faccombe. Tel: 026487 315

On the walk, this is a very local pub with its very own atmosphere and one that makes you feel immediately welcome. The owners take a great pride in their work which reflects in the accommodation.

Youth Hostel, Overton YHA, Overton. Tel: 0256 770516

Eight miles from the walk, this is a basic but pleasant hostel in what was once the village school. Set in the heart of the village, there are a number of good pubs within walking distance for your evening's entertainment. Camping is also permitted.

Camping and Caravanning

There are no obvious nearby sites.

THE BOW BEECH BOUND

Distance: 10¾ miles (17.25 km)
Time: Allow approximately 5 hours
Map: Ordnance Survey Landranger Map 197

Done a number of times. Master Robert — was closing down the last ...

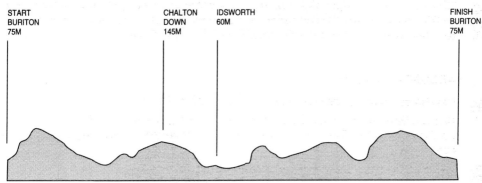

START
BURITON
75M

CHALTON
DOWN
145M

IDSWORTH
60M

FINISH
BURITON
75M

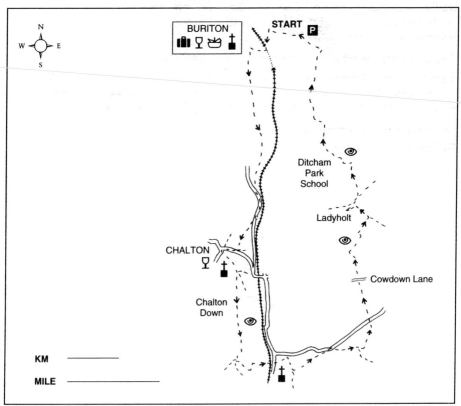

Walk Summary

One of my favourite walks in Hampshire, The Bow Beech Bound explores the very western tip of the South Downs. On a clear day you are rewarded with marvellous views of the sea as well as the downs. In the valleys the route passes through historic and picturesque villages. Be prepared for undulating terrain with one quite steep ascent and some muddy farm tracks. Most importantly, allow plenty of time to enjoy the scenery.

Start - OS. 740200 Map 197

The walk starts in front of the village church at Buriton, for traditionalists, the start or finish of the South Downs Way. The best approach is from the A3. From the north, unless you are joining the A3 at Petersfield, ignore both Petersfield turn offs, the second being to the industrial estate, to take the next turn off signposted to Buriton. At a roundabout turn right and follow the lane into the village of Buriton. Continue through the village until you see the village church ahead and a pond on your right. There is room for parking beside the church and pond. If coming from the south, take the first turn off signposted to Petersfield. Turn right to pass under the A3 and then, at a roundabout, continue straight on to follow the lane into Buriton. The nearest railway station is at Petersfield which is a mainline station. There is no obvious alternative start.

THE BOW BEECH BOUND

You will immediately be charmed by the village of Buriton, so well protected by its hanger.

i

Buriton (OS. 740200 Map 197) is used to walkers as before its extension the South Downs Way ended or started here. It is a good choice as in my mind, there is no finer village in Hampshire from which to start or end a walk. Looking about you, I am sure you will agree as did the Lakeland poet, Southey, who wrote a song in memory of Buriton's beauty.

The great church overlooking the pond was once also the parish church for Petersfield. Beside it and almost surrounding it, is the manor house which dates from the 13th century and where Edward Gibbon, author of "The Decline and Fall of the Roman Empire", once lived. Inside the church there is a souvenir from London. Round the font the original paving stones from London bridge form the floor. The village pond is fed by natural springs, the reason for the original settlement here which dates back to neolithic times.

To prepare you for your walk or as a treat at the finish, Buriton has two fine hostelries, The Master Robert Inn and The Five Bells. They are both free houses and compete to serve the best ale and food. The only solution therefore is to rest in each! For those who prefer to feast in the delights of the countryside, the village Post Office doubles as a general stores.

To start the walk, from the church take the signposted footpath which runs between the pond and church. This bends round behind the church and then right to meet a gate and stile, the original start and finish point of the South Downs Way. Cross the stile into a field and continue straight ahead ignoring a footpath off to the left and follow the white topped posts up the field. In front of you looms Buriton Hanger (hanger is the name for a steep tree clad slope) and to your right in a perfect position, an even more perfect cottage complete with pond, mock ruin and dovecot.

Continue uphill to meet a stile at the foot of the hanger, where it is worth stopping to look back over the village of Buriton. Cross over the stile and continue straight on following the footpath steeply uphill through the woods, to eventually bend right over a railway tunnel which is part of the main line between London and Portsmouth. Thereafter, continue climbing uphill and just before the top, look out for a narrow footpath on the right marked by a yellow arrow on a post, which you should take. If you continue uphill and meet a house, then you will have gone too far and should retrace your steps to find the footpath.

Follow the footpath through woodland along the side of the hill to soon pass a small ruined brick building on the left. Just after this, the footpath forks and you should take the left hand fork to shortly meet a narrow lane (part of the new South Downs Way extension). Turn right along the lane and shortly after passing a pair of gates on the left, turn left over a stile onto a signposted footpath. Take heed of the signs indicating you should keep to the path at all times as just off the path and concealed is a steep sided quarry.

The footpath leads gently uphill through woodland and as you progress, runs between distinctive banks before meeting a stile. Cross the stile and continue your route ahead to soon meet two wide tracks, one joining on either side, which continue ahead to form one large track. You should carry straight on along the track which takes you over the top of Head Down Plantation, blanketed by beautiful beech woods. As you progress, the woods thin out in places to afford views on your left across the valley to Ditcham Woods.

The track continues for approximately three quarters of a mile descending gradually, to eventually meet a wide crossing track. Here you should go over the crossing track to continue ahead on a now much narrower path, marked by yellow dots on some of the tree trunks. After a short distance you will meet and cross a stile into a field, after which you should carry straight on across the field heading for the electricity pilon ahead. The wooded hill to your right here is part of the Queen Elizabeth Forest, now a country park. The footpath across the field can be undefined. Accordingly, as you near the electricity pilon, follow the sweep of the field gently right passing to the right of the pilon and thereafter, bear left to pass under the wires between two pilons. As a guide, you should now be walking between the railway line on your left and a small lane on your right. Underfoot but not visible, is buried an ancient settlement inhabited between the 1st and 6th centuries AD.

Pass to the left of the second pilon and continue downhill heading roughly for the point where the railway line and lane appear almost to meet. As you near the far side of the field, look out for a stile on the right which you should cross to meet the lane. Turn left along the lane and follow it for approximately a quarter of a mile, until you come level with some old railway cottages on the left known as "Woodcroft Crossing" **(OS. 738166).** Here you should leave the lane to take a track right, which immediately runs uphill between banks. On nearing the top of the hill, Chalton Peak, the banks give way to open fields and there are good views left to what was once Lady Holt Park and Compton Down beyond. Looking back, you will also gain views over West Harting Down, featured in "10 Adventurous Walks in West Sussex". Just after, a windmill will also come into view ahead to your right. This stands on a hill overlooking Chalton village, our next destination.

The track eventually bends round to the right to meet a lane on to which you should turn right and follow it downhill. Just before a "T" junction, turn left alongside a small green to reach the centre of Chalton village.

Chalton (OS. 732160 Map 197) *cries out to be photographed. The thatched half timbered village inn, reputedly the oldest in Hampshire, sits below a perfectly rounded hill crowned by Chalton windmill. Opposite, a small green rises to the manor, the village church and a house, once a priory. The inn started life as a place to stay for privileged visitors to the church and manor. At the time, the manor was held by John O'Gaunt and it is from his crest that the inn takes its name. The inn is steeped in legend, most of them based around its chimney which has a priest hole, more cleverly concealed than most. There are stories of King Charles hiding here and a pint with a local, I am sure, would reveal many more. The inn is a worthy if not early place for a break. Apart from something tasty you can enjoy a sip of HSB (Horndean Special Brew), brewed by Gales no more than a couple of miles away, the other side of Windmill Down, in Horndean itself.*

On the village green once stood a whipping post and stocks, no doubt well used on those who left the inn after a drop too much! The church dates from the 12th century although it is known that there was a Saxon church before it. It is dedicated to St. Michael which is common of many churches built on a hillside. This stems from the belief of the defeat of Lucifer and his following of disloyal angels at the hand of St. Michael. Showing mercy, St. Michael allowed some of Lucifers' angels to live in the woods and hills.

Red Lion Chalton

Entry to the church is via an unusual but relatively modern porch. The original entrance was through the tower. Inside, the church boasts a decorative 15th century font. In the east wall there is an unusual window of four equal lights. They represent St. Michael, St. James and St. Hubert (two more local churches) and the fourth light represents St. George.

To continue our route, from "The Red Lion" inn take the footpath opposite which runs through the church yard. Pass to the left of the church entrance and cross a stile to continue ahead through the grave yard, often grazed by sheep, the traditional method of keeping the grass down. At the far side, you should pass through a small wooden gate into an extension of the grave yard and follow a narrow footpath which cuts across the right hand corner to meet a stile. Cross the stile and follow the path ahead which bends gently round to the left to soon meet another stile. Go over the stile immediately after which, you will meet three footpaths which fan out in front of you across a field. You should take the right hand path and go uphill across the field following the marker poles for guidance.

The path you are following goes over the top of Chalton Down which is 145 metres high, the top being marked by an old burial mound or tumulus. From here you will enjoy some of the best views on the walk. Ahead of you are Emsworth and Chichester harbour and beyond, on a clear day, the Isle of Wight. To your right is Portsdown Hill and its unusual hill forts and left, the South Downs and Stanstead Forest. Behind you, rises Butser Hill and the wooded West Harting Down.

From the burial mound continue straight on, heading for an electricity pilon slightly to your left at the left hand perimeter of the field. Pass to the right of the pilon and shortly after, look out for a stile on your left. Cross over the stile and turn right along a track to follow the right hand perimeter of a field, which overlooks the hamlet of Idsworth in the valley below. Eventually, you will meet a crossing track signposted as a bridleway, onto which you should turn left. This takes you across the centre of a field and continues downhill to meet a "T" junction, where you should bend left in the direction of the bridleway sign and soon after, right to continue your descent. You will soon arrive at a small cluster of houses and as such, the centre of Idsworth.

Carry straight on passing between some cottages on your right and a farm on the left and as the driveway to the farm bends right, ignore this to continue ahead and pass through a metal gate to cross the railway line. Take great care as this is the main line between London and Portsmouth. At the other side of the railway line, continue straight on passing to the right of an old railway cottage to meet a lane. Look out for an old post box on your right at this point.

Cross the lane and follow a grass path ahead which leads up to St. Huberts Chapel. At the start of the path there is a small wooden bridge, built to allow access in heavy rains when the path is liable to flooding. The chapel is protected by a wooden fence, a kissing gate providing access.

St. Huberts Chapel (OS. 743137 Map 197) is a jewel in any county. Its simplicity and lonely position, part of its beauty, also hide its royal heritage. St. Huberts was originally built by Earl Godwin, father of King Harold who was later to lose this land to the Normans. It is believed that Edward the Confessor who held the manor of Idsworth, used St. Huberts as a hunting chapel. This explains the chapel's dedication, St. Hubert being the patron Saint of hunters. Some early murals on the north wall of the chancel depict St. Hubert in a hunting scene restoring a man who believed he was a wolf to human form. Another, represents the feast of Herod with the head of John the Baptist, the martyr, being presented to Salome. The paintings date from around 1300 and are some of the best of their kind in the country. Another unusual feature is the original Norman window in the north wall. Try and imagine the whole chapel being lit by these.

To continue our route, turn left immediately before the kissing gate and follow the fencing around to the rear of the chapel. Here you should join a footpath which goes diagonally left across the field to reach a stile at the far side. Cross the stile and turn right in the direction of the footpath sign, to follow the right hand perimeter of the next field downhill.

At the corner of the field, follow the field perimeter around to the left and ignore a turning off to the right. As you round the field corner, note the hollow on your right which was probably once a chalk well, a regular feature in this part of the country. Chalk wells were used to bring good chalk or lime to the surface to fertilise the fields. They were often dug at the base of hills and could be as deep as eighty feet. To get at the best chalk, several short tunnels would be dug from the central shaft. As the wells fell into disuse, the land around them collapsed to form a shallow hollow, such as the one we see here. In later years farmers dug open pits or created small quarries, of which the South Downs has many.

The footpath continues along the right hand perimeter of the field following the base of a hill. In line with "Old Idsworth Farm" in the distance on the left, the path passes through a gap in a line of trees to enter the next field and continues along the right hand perimeter, following a line of newly planted beech trees.

The footpath soon almost meets a lane on the left. Here you should turn right along a signposted footpath to go uphill and enter the tree line. After a short steep climb you will reach a track on to which you should turn left, which continues to climb albeit along a much gentler incline. Soon after, you should look out for a footpath sign on your right which can at times be hidden by the leafy foliage through which you are passing. Here you should leave the track, going up a small bank, to turn left along the footpath which continues uphill winding through a mixture of hazel, fir, yew and sycamore. Here the wood gives the appearance of having once been managed estate land, with much of it specially planted.

On nearing the top of the hill pass another footpath sign, which acts as confirmation that you are on the right route. Soon after, the path bends right beside a field on your right and for a short time, we pass into West Sussex. The path continues its gentle climb now following the field perimeter and soon meets a "T" junction. Turn left here along a track signposted as a bridleway, which can be extremely muddy in wet weather. Stay on the track as it continues through the wood until you meet a fork. Take the left hand and more prominent track, still signposted as a bridleway and after a short distance ignore a signposted footpath off to the right. The track you are on now widens and begins to go downhill running through a grove of yew trees.

After the yew trees the track meets a field which you should cross by way of a well defined bridleway, across the centre to reach a lane. Turn right along the lane for approximately thirty paces and then left onto a signposted bridleway which runs initially through a thin strip of woodland. The bridleway then continues through a gateway and across the centre of a field. At the far side, you should stay on the bridleway to pass through a hedgerow and continue straight on across the next field. At the far side, stay on the bridleway to continue ahead, going over a crossing track, Cowdown Lane, into a third field where again you should go straight across the centre.

At the end of the third field, continue ahead along a narrow path which winds through another strip of woodland to pass through a small wooden gate into another field. Here you should bear right to meet a pair of metal farm gates. Do not go through the gates, but turn left in front of them to follow the field perimeter round, until you eventually meet a second pair of metal gates. Pass through the gates and continue ahead, ignoring a track off to the left and follow the right hand perimeter of the field.

Half way across the field you will pass some mounds which make up a reservoir. From here you can enjoy more good views which include two prominent buildings to your left, "Ditcham Park School" and ahead to your right, "Uppark House", where H.G. Wells stayed as a boy. "Uppark" is now in the hands of the National Trust.

Follow the track along field perimeters to its end where you will meet a gravel track at a "T" junction (OS. 758166). If you were to turn right, the track would lead to the hamlet of Eckensfield which is visible. Our route however, is left along the track heading for "Ditcham Park School" in the distance at the other side of the valley. Stay on the track as it bends left ignoring another track off to the right and continue heading for some cottages known as Lady Holt. The name refers to the original house, "Lady Holt Park", which stood roughly on this site and was once home to the writer, John Caryll. The land through which we are passing was part of the estate. In 1747 a brutal murder occurred here, the victim was an Excise Officer called Galley. He was killed by a rough gang of smugglers known as The Hawkhurst Gang (see "10 Adventurous Walks in West Sussex" - Smugglers Seven).

As the track bends left again to enter the properties, you should leave it to turn right, almost back on yourself, along a signposted public bridleway which goes downhill into Harehurst Wood. At the bottom of the valley, the track bends left in front of an old concrete pond and immediately after, passes through a gate to meet a wide grass track which is also part of the Sussex Border Path. Turn right along the track and follow it as it bends round to the left, ignoring another track off to the right. This is a beautiful part of the walk in all seasons and an area where you may be lucky in catching a glimpse of the many deer which live here.

After some distance, the track forks and you should ignore the more prominent track off to the right to continue ahead along a signposted public bridleway. This soon meets a wide crossing track which you should ignore to carry straight on in the direction of the public bridleway sign, to shortly meet a beautiful steep sided valley. Follow the bridleway which bends sharply left to climb up the side of the valley along the edge of the wood. At the top stay on the path as it bends right to run between fields. Here you get the best views of the valley and at the bottom, the appropriately named "Downley Farm".

After a short distance, the bridleway bends left again and then gently right to soon meet a track where you should continue ahead. (Do not turn right). The track also runs between fields heading towards "Ditcham Park School", now visible on your left and ends at the school drive way. Turn right going away from the school along the drive and follow this for approximately three hundred metres, until you meet a strip of woodland on your left with a path running beside it, signposted as a public bridleway.Turn left onto the bridleway which soon leads to a wide track which is the start of Ditcham Wood.

Turn right on to the track passing a Forestry Commission sign on your left for Ditcham Wood and follow the track, which is marked by blue topped posts, for a short distance. Look out for a narrow path off to the left, again marked by blue topped posts and a horseshoe, which you should take to wind through the very picturesque beech woods. You will soon meet a crossing track which you should ignore to continue ahead along the same narrow path through the woods. Your route is still marked by the now familiar blue topped posts.

The path leads gently downhill through the beech woods and eventually exits the wood beside another Forestry Commission sign. You should continue along the path, now along the edge of the wood with fields on your left, to later lead out to a narrow lane which is also part of the South Downs Way. Directly to your left here is "Coulters Dean Farm", almost hidden and set in a superb position.

Bear right along the lane following the South Downs Way until the lane bends right. Here you should leave it to follow a track on the left downhill, signposted as a cart track and to Buriton. The track is known locally as The Milky Way, a reference I feel, to the cows that once used it and not to heavenly bodies! The track leads gently downhill passing under some electricity pilons and shortly after, bends right to continue more steeply downhill between banks.

At the bottom of the hill as the track bends right, look out for a stile and signposted footpath on your left. Go over the stile into a field and cross the field following a line of white topped posts, heading for the familiar sight of Buriton in the distance. At the far side, you will recognise the stile which we crossed at the beginning of the walk. Go over this once more and retrace your steps to the church from where we started.

ACCOMMODATION

Master Robert Inn, Buriton. Tel: 0730 267275

A couple of hundred yards from the walk, this friendly free house has just had its rooms refurbished to offer a high standard of accommodation. The inn itself is divided into an informal bar and a good quality restaurant. The bar is a favourite haunt for people doing the South Downs Way.

Barrow Hill Farm, Ramsdean. Tel: 073087 340

Three miles from the walk, the owners have virtually given over their farmhouse to their guests. The rooms are excellently furnished with quality antiques. A comfortable stay is guaranteed.

Youth Hostel, Portsmouth YHA, Cosham. Tel: 0705 375661

Approximately sixteen miles from the walk, it is perhaps surprising to find a youth hostel so far from the start of such a popular long distance trail. The youth hostel itself is an old manor house in a busy Portsmouth suburb.

Camping and Caravanning

There are no camping or caravan sites in the immediate vicinity. Hayling Island however, ten miles south, is a popular holiday centre and as such, has a wide choice of sites. For information on these, contact the Havant Tourist Office, tel: 0705 480024.

A LOVELY WALK — 08/07/2017

THE DANEBURY TEST

Distance: 11 miles (18 km)

Time: Allow approximately 5½ hours, more if you wish to visit Danebury Hill Fort

Map: Ordnance Survey Landranger Map 185

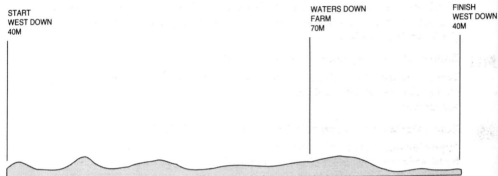

START
WEST DOWN
40M

WATERS DOWN
FARM
70M

FINISH
WEST DOWN
40M

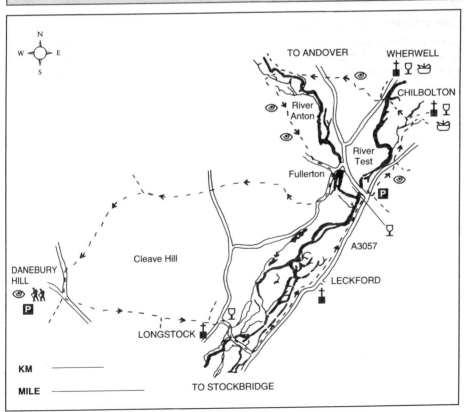

Walk Summary

Approximately two thirds of the walk is through the valleys of the Anton and Test, with one third leaving the tranquility of these Hampshire rivers to follow prehistoric tracks in search of Danebury Hill Fort, high on a chalk ridge. Apart from the obvious attraction of the rivers and hill fort, the route passes through or close to some of the most picturesque villages in Hampshire, rich in Saxon thatch. There are several good hostelries en route, so ensure you start out early!

Start - OS. 384390 Map 185

The walk starts from a parking area at the bottom of West Down at Chilbolton. If coming from the north, from Andover take the A3057 south and just after the road passes over the river Test beside the Mayfly pub on the right, take the next turning left, signposted to Chilbolton. Immediately after this, turn first right into the parking area for West Down. If coming from the south, from Stockbridge take the A3057 north. Approximately three quarters of a mile after passing through Leckford, the road bends sharp left to cross over the river Test. Do not follow the road left, but turn off here to continue straight on following the signs for Chilbolton. As above, immediately after this turn first right into the car park for West Down. An alternative start may be made from the car park at Danebury Hill Fort (OS. 330378 Map 185). The nearest railway station is at Andover from where you can get a bus to Chilbolton.

THE DANEBURY TEST

From the parking area at the foot of West Down, head back towards the road just before which you should turn right to follow a green arrow uphill, part of the Test Way. The footpath takes you across the side of West Down, where you should ignore any turnings off to the right which lead to the summit. As you progress you will enjoy good views behind over the Test valley.

West Down (OS. 385392 Map 185) has signs of habitation dating from neolithic times. Several ancient tracks, namely the Mark Way linking with the Harrow Way and the Celtic Road pass over the down and another crosses the Test towards Danebury, part of which we will follow later. The dwellings on West Down are older that those of Danebury Hill Fort. Here the people lived in pits and did not feel the need for fortification, something which did not develop until the iron age with the coming of the Celts. One of the pits nearest the river appears to have been a cooking pit as it was found full of burned animal bones. The fields to the east of West Down are rich in flint tools and hammer stones.

The path gradually becomes more prominent and runs through a wooded scrubland area and thereafter, a mixture of wood and open downland which in summer is a picture, covered by chalkland flowers. After passing an old iron seat on your right the path begins to descend and eventually leads down to a concrete drive. Turn left along the drive to meet a road where you should turn left again for approximately twenty paces. Cross the road and follow the public footpath sign ahead into a small grass clearing with seating overlooking the river Test. Bear right to leave the clearing and join a narrow fenced footpath running parallel with the river on your left. As you descend, you will enjoy views over the river and in particular a superb garden with fish pools and a thatched summer house.

The footpath then runs through a small area of woodland and crosses over a concrete drive shortly after, to continue along the right hand bank of the Test. This eventually leads you out to a cricket and playing field, where you should bear left to follow the perimeter, marked by green arrows on a white background indicating you are following the Test Way. Just before you reach the pavillion, look out for a small footpath on the left going over a stile. Cross the stile and follow the footpath right where you will find yourself in the Test valley proper. To your left the river Test winds through unspoilt water meadows, water meadows which as far back as records exist, have never been ploughed or treated with chemicals. The result is a landscape rich in rare plants and insects and frequented by endless varieties of waterfowl.

The path soon joins a gravel drive at a cottage, where you should bear left to follow the drive passing in front of the cottage and continue until you meet another gravel drive. Here you should bear left. If you wish to visit the village of Chilbolton however, then take the lane ahead for a short detour.

Chilbolton (OS. 395400 Map 185) is a curious mixture of old and new. Recently the grave of a neolithic chieftan was discovered in the village. Many of the thatched cottages date from the 17th and 18th centuries and yet on the hill behind Chilbolton, there is a huge radio telescope (run by the Science Research Council), the ultimate in 20th century technology. Before the radio telescope, the hill was home to an aerodrome once used for test flights on the famous Spitfire. The aerodrome was also used in the Second World War by the 17th Airborn (US) Para and Glider Troopers. It was from here men were flown to take part in the Battle of the Bulge, in which tragically so many people lost their lives. To remember these men, the face of the town hall is decorated with the stars and stripes topped by a gilt eagle. Inside the hall hangs an American flag, the flag had been flown for a day in Washington in Chilbolton's honour.

Bringing you back to the present, the village has a Post Office doubling as a general stores and a respectable pub, The Abbots Mitre, a free house. The village church is at the northern end.

Our route is, as mentioned, left along a gravel drive and shortly after over a very shallow ford and footbridge. Immediately after, you should bear left across the grass along a fairly well defined path. Go over a grass clearing often used as a parking area and follow a well trodden path ahead to pass over the river Test by way of a narrow bridge. At the other side, ignore a path going off to the left and continue ahead across the water meadows, ignoring any further minor paths.

At the other side of the water meadows cross another bridge, this time wooden and note the gated bridleway on your right where riders must go to cross the river. The wooden bridge soon gives way to a small tarmac path and then another wooden bridge which crosses the main flow of the river. Take time here to enjoy your surroundings and perhaps overcome your envy of the inhabitants of the pretty thatched cottages at the water's edge. If you are lucky, you might even see a salmon which have been known to come this far up river.

At the other side of the river, follow the footpath ahead to reach a lane. If you are in need of early refreshments, turn right here to visit Wherwell village.

Wherwell (OS. 390409 Map 185) is one of those picture postcard villages of half timbered cottages and Saxon thatch. All around you is peace and tranquility and yet Wherwell more than most Hampshire villages, is steeped in tragedy and legend. Most of it stems from the ruined Saxon priory on the banks of the Test. The priory was founded in 986 AD by King Edgar's widow, Elfrida, during the reign of her son, King Ethelred the

Unready. Her son had come to the throne following the murder of her stepson, King Edward the Martyr at Corfe Castle in Dorest. It is now known that it was Elfrida who had plotted King Edward's murder.

Elfrida was associated with several other murders and with the help of King Edgar, even murdered her own husband, the Earl Aetholwald one of the king's courtiers, to enable her to marry the king himself. It is reputed that Elfrida was a woman of great beauty and determination and used her charms well to further her own cause. Eventually, her conscience caught up with her and she built the priory as a recluse and lived there almost as a hermit reflecting, it is said, on her past ill deeds. Queen Elfrida eventually died by drowning in the Test, ending her life as dramatically as she had lived it.

The priory was later ruled by the Abbess Edith, wife of Edward the Confessor, who did much to right the reputation of the priory making it a convent of some renown. After being ransacked by King Stephan, the building was later restored to become an abbey ruled by a revered woman, Blessed Euphemia. The abbey's life eventually came to an abrupt end with the dissolution of the monasteries under King Henry VIII. The only remains of the abbey today, are in the west end of the church. These consist of a figure of Euphemia and some stone figures representing the "harrowing of hell" (Christ's descent into hell). Today, a private house stands in the grounds, home to the Countess of Brecknock.

The church after the abbey, is a relatively modern building, though it does have traces of Norman architecture. Apart from the relics from the abbey, it has a memorial stone to a nun from Wherwell priory. The nun's name was Frithburya and literally means "pledge of peace". For some years the stone was mislaid and was eventually found being used as a platform for a bell ringer.

At the centre of the village is The White Lion, a Whitbread pub and an old coaching inn. During the Civil War it is said that the roundheads attacking a royalist stronghold at the priory, mistakenly fired a cannonball at The White Lion. The cannonball was fired too high and dropped down the pub's chimney. It now hangs outside. Not surprisingly, with such a turbulant history, Wherwell is steeped in mystery and legend. The village abounds with tales of witches and ghosts, in fact even the village name is derived from "Hwerwyl" meaning "cauldron springs". One of the most well known legends is that of the cockatrice. The story goes that a duck laid an egg in the abbey cript which was hatched by a toad. The result was a cockatrice, a kind of dragon. The cockatrice would take people from the village to its lair in the abbey for food. Eventually, a man named Green defeated the cockatrice by tricking it into fighting its reflection until it died of exhaustion. As a reward the village gave Green a gift of four acres of land and an area in Harewood Forest is still to this day known as Green's Acres.

Another legend, is that of the Romsey nuns who came to the valley looking for refuge at the nunnery from the marauding Danes. Unfortunately, they lost their way and ended up dying in the surrounding woods. Before they died however, they reproached the Almighty for their fate and thus lost their souls, which turned into wild cats still said to roam the area today. If you decide to stay overnight at Wherwell, perhaps at The White Lion, take a wander down to the church yard where, apart from the wild cats, you may see lights glowing between the gravestones. These are knowns as corpses' lights, though it has been suggested they may be nothing more than glow worms which are common in this part of the valley. On the other hand, you may decide to stay in the pub for another drink to contemplate the many legends!

Apart from murders, a cockatrice and glowing corpses, the village has a down to earth general stores selling all types of provisions to prepare the walker for the next encounter.

Our route however is, left along the lane in the direction of the Test Way signs. After approximately fifty metres, turn right on to a signposted footpath, still marked by the green arrow of the Test Way and go uphill. After a short distance, you will reach a "T" junction. The path leading off to the right here is another route into the village of Wherwell. Our route is left over a stile, thereby leaving the Test Way, into a field where you should continue straight ahead, keeping to the left hand perimeter. The perimeter gradually bends right at which point you will pass an old brick bridge on the left, a remnant of the disused railway line which connected Andover to the Longparish branch line at Fullerton.

The path you are now on joins another which comes in from the left from under the bridge just mentioned. Here you should maintain your route along the field perimeter now following a track leading uphill. Someway up the hill, follow the track as it bends left still climbing though affording views back over the Test valley. The white buildings visible above the trees are the radio telescopes at Chilbolton mentioned earlier.

At the top of the hill after perhaps stopping to regain your breath and admire the view, stay on the track as it bends right to run between hedgerows. The track narrows as you continue to soon become just a path which then bends left to enter a field with now very different views ahead. Bear right at this point to follow the right hand perimeter of the field, at the end of which is a small wooden gate through which you should pass. Continue ahead still on the path, now traversing open hillside until you meet a fork. Take the right hand fork thereby maintaining your route, until you meet a bridleway sign beside a fence on your right. Here you should bear diagonally left to go steeply downhill until you reach a farm gate. Take care at this point as this part of the walk can be particularly slippery in wet weather. (STRAIGHT DOWN TO GATE)

Pass through the gate to meet a road, the A3057. Cross the road and pass through a metal farm gate the other side into a field and continue straight on along the left hand perimeter. This is marked as a bridleway. At the far side, pass through another metal gate and immediately after, turn left to follow a signposted footpath through a wooded area which can be fairly overgrown in summer. This leads out to a bridge over which you should pass to cross the river Anton. This is a tranquil spot and a good place to rest for a while.

At the other side of the bridge, turn right to follow the river bank which bears left and then right beside a stile. You should ignore the stile and leave the river at this point to continue straight on heading for some trees. At the trees, cross over a small brick bridge which passes over another arm of the Anton river and go through a metal gate into a small field. Go straight across the field and pass through a kissing gate beside a farm gate the other side, to lead out onto a track which was once the railway line from Andover to Fullerton.

Turn left here and follow the track, shortly after ignoring another track off to the right. As you progress you will gain good views left across the Anton valley and the earlier part of the walk. This view suddenly ends by way of a hedgerow on the left with a field opening out on the right. Soon after, you should look out for a footpath sign on your right pointing across the field which you should now follow. The footpath goes diagonally left uphill across the field. If this appears undefined, then head for the left hand corner of the wood ahead.

☀ BLOCKED BY GATE TURN Ⓡ INTO FIELD

→ GOES THROUGH STILE BY METAL GATE

On reaching the woodland take time to stop for a rest and enjoy the views back, where in the distance the buildings of Andover are now visible. Follow the perimeter of the woodland on your right uphill to the end of the field and pass through a gap in the hedge to continue ahead. Follow the right hand perimeter of the next field and ignore a track off to your right. As you continue you will enjoy some of the best views over the Test and Anton valleys as well as the radio telescopes mentioned earlier. At the far side of the field, the path becomes a track and you should continue straight on along the ridge of the hill.

The track eventually bends right to meet a lane, where you should turn left to follow the lane downhill. Pass a farm and then ignore a track off to the right and continue until you meet another lane on the right, signposted to Longstock. Our route is right here, but first it is worth continuing ahead for a few hundred metres to discover the beautiful "Fullerton Mill" on the river Anton.

Continuing on our route, take the lane signposted to Longstock and follow this passing "Fullerton Grange" on your right. After approximately half a mile, you will see a track on your right signposted as a byway (OS. 375389). The lane (which is not our route from here) continues to "Longstock Park", famous for its water gardens. The gardens are open between April and September on the third Sunday of each month and if you have time are well worth a visit.

Returning to our route, take the signposted byway right. You are now treading one of the ancient Wessex tracks, used by man probably since prehistoric times. This particular track connected Danebury Fort with West Down and beyond. The track leads up through a valley and you should later ignore a stile on the left to continue straight on. It then gradually bends left skirting the steep sides of Hazel Down on your left, where our ancestors who built the track once grew their crops. Eventually, the track meets a lane which you should cross to follow the track ahead now signposted as a right of way. From here, we get our first view of Danebury hill fort, it is the distinctive tree covered hill ahead to your left.

The track which is now extremely wide passes under a line of electricity pilons, where soon after to your left is the prominent grass hillside of Cleave Hill and at its foot, "Charity Down Farm". When I last walked this way in summer, a grass track leading off to Cleave Hill was an absolute picture, lined by corn, poppies and other wild summer flowers. Either side of the track now, the people from the hill fort once buried their dead. Unfortunately, the graves here have now fallen to the plough and only the width of the track indicates the importance this route once held for the fort's inhabitants. (NO LOU THERE

Stay on the main track, ignoring all turnings off to eventually pass over a cattle grid after which the track becomes much narrower. The track now begins to bend left still heading towards Danebury Hill fort and soon meets a larger track which is in fact the drive way to "Charity Down Farm". Do not turn left, but continue ahead along the track where ahead of you now is a smaller tree topped hill, known as The Turret. NOW HOUSE AND NOW CALLED

You will eventually pass an old stone barn on your right, "Waters Down Farm", just before meeting a lane. Turn left to follow the lane uphill, where as you continue you will pass an old tree covered mound on your left, one of the few remaing burial mounds. Shortly after, you will reach a "T" junction. A signpost indicates that turning right here takes you to Danebury Ring and Grateley. Although our route is not to Danebury Ring, after following such an ancient track for the last hour, I feel it only fitting that we should visit the home of the people who first used it. Following the road right for a few hundred

LONG SECTION (d) 2½ - 3 MILES

metres will take you to the entrance of Danebury Ring or hill fort. If however, you wish to continue our walk uuniterupted, then turn left instead to join a track. (CHURCH ROAD) LEADS TO LONGSTOCK

Danebury Hill Fort, 143m/469 ft (OS. 324377 Map 185), stands proud in a region which had one of the densest populations of iron age people in Europe. From the hill fort itself, six other hill forts in Hampshire can be seen and some more in Wiltshire. Up until the coming of the Celts England as it was, was a relatively peaceful place and the need for defences was unrealised. The Celts however were a warlike people and although they brought new technology, they also brought with them tribal hatreds and the first hill forts quickly developed to protect the local populations. As the years went by, Celtic life became more organised and these forts were more carefully constructed, with a sense of co-operation with nearby forts to defend themselves against a potential common enemy. This eventually arrived in the form of the Roman conquest.

Danebury was built about 550 BC, the fort being enclosed by one simple circular bank and a timber rampart. Over the centuries, the fort was improved and the defences became more complicated. At its height, Danebury would have protected around one thousand people and was the finest hill fort in the region. Since excavation started in 1969, a number of weapons used by the fort's warlike inhabitants have been found. Amongst them, spears, swords, knives, the remains of shields and most common of all, sling stones of which thousands were found. The sling was the most popular weapon and was especially useful in defending the fort when close combat weapons could not be used. Amongst the prize spoils of war were their opponents heads, these would be hacked from the bodies of their victims and errected on poles around the fort to warn off potential attackers. It is believed that the heads of important enemies were preserved in cedar oil and kept in the chieftan's house to be shown off to visitors. To testify to Danebury's strength, many severed heads were discovered during the excavation.

Although warlike, the Celts were also deeply superstitious and had a wide variety of Gods. Perhaps understandably, many of their superstitions and charms related to battle. The famous Torc is of Celtic origin, this was a band of ornate metal worn around the kneck and was said to ward off danger. Each settlement had a Druid and apart from the chieftan, he was the most powerful man in the fort. The Celts also believed in the afterlife and in keeping with their warlike tendencies, a warrior's most prized weapons would be buried with him or her to carry on their ways after death. The numerous Gods of the Celts were believed to reside on Earth, generally at springs and rivers, amongst rocks and in clumps of trees, usually on a hill. It is a peculiar phenomenom that since the Celts demise, many of their hill forts, including Danebury are now prominent clumps of trees. At these sacred sites, offerings were often made which mostly included the gift of fine weaponry. Animals were also sacrificed to the Gods, in particular the legs of a horse appear to have been of great significance.

Life at Danebury came to a sudden end around 100 BC and probably ended in the same way as the fort had reached its prominence, in battle. To testify to this, the excavation has revealed that the main gate had been burned to the ground. Standing amongst the peaceful trees which now inhabit the fort, it is hard to imagine the noisy life that once existed here and the numerous battles including the final one that saw the burning of the main gate and the undoubted massacre which followed.

With more questions than answers, it is probably time to return to our route. If Danebury has aroused your interest in Celtic life, then I recommend a visit to the Museum of the Iron Age at Andover (Tel: 0264 66283) and Butser Archeological Farm, south of

Petersfield, where an iron age farm has been recreated. For more information telephone: 0705 598838.

Back at the "T" junction, to continue our route, you must turn left to join a track signposted as a byway heading away from the hill fort. This track is known to be one of the most ancient in the country and connected Danebury Fort with Woolbury, the other side of the Test, from where it continues to St. Catherines hill fort at Winchester and then on to Old Winchester Hill and Butser Hill from where it links the hill forts along the South Downs (now the South Downs Way).

The track climbs gently uphill and is lined in summer with a mass of hedges and brambles. At the brow of the hill you will pass a series of brick and flint barns on your right and see ahead of you the Test valley. Stay on the track to begin a long gentle descent, ignoring a footpath sometime on off to your right. The track eventually becomes tarmac and continues a now more steep descent to soon graduate into a lane passing between the houses of Longstock village. Ignore a signposted footpath off to the left and continue to meet a "T" junction beside St. Mary's church, the centre of Longstock village.

Longstock (OS. 360371 Map 185) *is a peaceful village on the west banks of the Test. Its pub, The Peat Spade Inn (Gales Ales), remembers the practice which allowed farm workers one day off in a year to cut peat which they then sold or used as fuel. The church is of fairly recent construction being built on the site of a former Saxon church. Apart from a six hundred year old font there is nothing of striking interest. The church's greatest asset, like the village, is its beauty.*

Turn left to pass a line of beautiful thatched cottages until you arrive at "The Peat Spade Inn". Turn right beside the pub and follow the lane out of the village to wind back across the Test valley. Today, the lane provides an easy crossing. In the past however, the crossing was treacherous and many people died by wandering off the route and sinking in the bogs. To try and prevent such tragedy, the way was marked by stakes and it is from this that Longstock has derived its name, Longstock literally meaning "places with stakes". Continuing, perhaps for once thankful of modern technology, you will soon pass another lovely cottage on your right, "Willows" where the lane meets one of the arms of the river Test.

The lane bends gently to cross the river where to your left there is a thatched hut, a fishing hut topped by an interesting weather vein, surrounded by a mass of reeds and bull rushes and very much a haven for wildfowl. This beautiful landscape is one of the most photographed in the Test valley and the hut appears on the cover of numerous tourist brochures. Behind the hut hidden in the reeds, are the remains of a Danish dock. A few steep banks are all that remain of a dock which once harboured many Danish longboats. The dock was not only designed to harbour boats but also to protect them from attack. It is very possible that the fleet of ships harboured here belonged to

Fishing Hut

King Cnute who is known to have sailed up the Test, burning Romsey to the ground.

Stay on the lane to cross two more smaller bridges over different arms of the Test to begin a gentle climb towards a bridge over another disused railway line. Just before the bridge however, turn right on to a footpath which is signposted to Stockbridge. This leads you down to the old railway line itself where you should turn left.

You will now follow the old railway line thus rejoining the Test Way to our starting point, a distance of approximately two miles. The line follows the west bank of the river Test and in summer is a mass of colourful flowers supporting a wealth of insects and in particular, butterflies. The beauty of this line was recognised by Queen Victoria who insisted travelling this way when visiting Southampton.

At one point on the footpath, the undergrowth gives way on your right to allow views across to Leckford village. This village is wholly owned by the John Lewis Partnership who purchased it in 1928. The partnership also owns approximately seven miles of the river Test which together make up the Leckford Estate. Every house in Leckford is inhabited either by a partner or pensioner of the John Lewis Partnership and the fishing rights, along with a golf course, are also open to all partners.

You should continue to follow the old railway line passing under a number of bridges, until eventually you cross a small wooden footbridge over a stream flowing into the Test. On your left now, you will spot "The Mayfly" pub. Pass under a red brick bridge and immediately after, turn right following the green arrow of the Test Way. This will take you over another small footbridge to follow a red brick wall on your left uphill, to arrive at a road opposite the parking area from where our walk commenced.

Before leaving it is worth visiting "The Mayfly" pub, Wayside Inns, which has a beautiful garden on the banks of the Test. Here you can sit with a well earned drink watching the peaceful waters of the Test and reflect on the turbulant past which the valley hides so well.

ACCOMMODATION

The White Lion, Wherwell. Tel: 0264 860317

A quarter of a mile from the walk, this historic inn is the ideal place to stay if you really want to soak up the atmosphere of the Test valley. The inn compliments one of the most picturesque villages in Hampshire and is a real treat after a hard day's walking.

The Great Barn, Nether Wallop. Tel: 0264 782142

Three and a half miles from the walk, this beautiful B&B is set in a building of historic interest.

Youth Hostel, Overton YHA, Overton. Tel: 0256 770516

Eleven miles from the walk, this is a basic but pleasant hostel in what was once the village school. Set in the heart of the village, there are a number of good pubs within walking distance for your evening's entertainment. Camping is also permitted.

Camping and Caravanning, Wyke Down Touring Park, Picket Piece. Tel: 0264 352048

Five and a half miles from the walk, this seven acre site has just about every amenity you could want.

THE HIGH HANGER HIKE

Distance: 11 miles (18 km)

Time: Allow approximately 5 hours

Map: Ordnance Survey Landranger Map 186

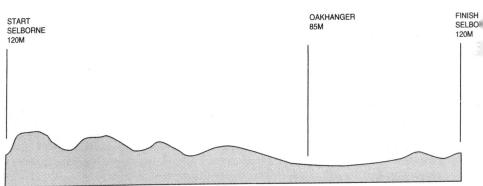

START
SELBORNE
120M

OAKHANGER
85M

FINISH
SELBO
120M

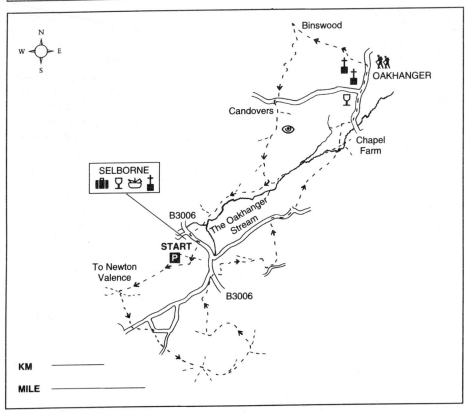

Walk Summary

The High Hanger Hike takes you through countryside that Gilbert White, the renound 18th century naturalist, wrote so fondly of. Although there have been in places some startling changes since then, much of the walk Gilbert White would still recognise if he were still alive today. A great deal of the route follows the famous Hampshire hangers, hanger being an old Hampshire description for a steep tree covered slope. Apart from the start, there are no extreme ascents, however parts of the route can be extremely muddy so make sure you have the right gear.

Start - OS. 743336 Map 186

The walk starts from the public car park behind "The Selborne Arms" pub. Selborne itself is situated on the B3006 between Alton on the A31 and Greatham on the A325, though if you are coming from the Greatham direction it is more likely you will be approaching via the newly built A3. If this is the case, you must leave the A3 when you see the signs for Alton. There is a choice of two railway stations, one at Alton and one at Liss. From either you can take a bus to Selborne. An alternative starting point is at Shortheath (OS. 770364) which enables you to make Selborne a good lunch time refuelling point.

THE HIGH HANGER HIKE

From the car park take the footpath going up beside it, signposted to the Zig Zag and Hanger. This leads you gently uphill with a line of trees on your right and a field on your left with the tree covered slopes of Selborne Common ahead. Ignore a path off to the left and continue ahead, passing through a kissing gate to meet a National Trust sign for Selborne Common and a collection box. After the gate, take the turning left signposted as the Zig Zag to ascend what is the beginning of numerous steps up the side of Selborne Hanger. As you continue, you will quickly realise the reason for the name, Zig Zag!

The Zig Zag which was built by Gilbert White and his brother in 1753, affords excellent views as you continue. Almost two thirds of the way up you will reach a bench for a rest should you need it. There are paths here leading off to the left and right which you should ignore to continue your climb up the Zig Zag. At the very top of the hill you will arrive at another bench beside a large stone, this is known as the Wishing Stone and nine times out of ten most peoples' first wish is probably that there is no more Zig Zag to climb! The stone was actually placed here in 1768, though from where it actually originates is open to debate. Apart from making a wish, the views here are also worth stopping for, with "Wick Hill Farm" directly ahead on the hill opposite and to the right slightly, two modern radar balls, the larger of which we will pass later on the walk.

Standing with the bench behind you looking at the view, turn right and then right again thereby walking behind the bench to take a path right leading to Selborne Common. You should now have a hedgerow on your left and follow the path ahead ignoring any minor turnings. This becomes more prominent as you continue with the hedgerow gradually disappearing on your left, to make way for the common itself. The path, known as the Pipe Line, now crosses the centre of Selborne Common which is made up of beautiful deciduous woodland interspersed by wild grassland. It is easy to understand why Gilbert White loved to study the common.

After some distance, the woodland opens out to a more prominent grassland area dotted with gorse and bracken. The sight of the gorse reminds me of a story that I think you

27

will enjoy. Gorse or furze as it was once known, was commonly used to plug holes in hedges as well as being a popular food for fire. Too lazy to cut their own gorse to burn, some folk often used to steal it from the hedgerow. One farmer fed up with this, hollowed out one piece of gorse and packed it with gunpowder. The unfortunate thief who looked forward to a roaring fire, ended up having his house blown clean away!

Soon after, you will meet a fork where you should follow the left hand path, thereby remaining on the more prominent path. You should ignore any minor paths or tracks off to the left or right. At the far side of the common you will eventually meet a wide crossing track, which you should cross to shortly meet a National Trust sign at a junction of paths and tracks. Ahead of you, for guidance, is a wooden fence and beyond, an open field and a house complete with tennis court. Should you wish to take a detour into the village of Newton Valance, then follow the bridleway ahead.

i   *Newton Valance (OS. 724327 Map 186) is one of those forgotten corners of England. In true english form an elegant church provides a place of worship for the inhabitants of the manor, which shares its drive. At the end of the drive waits a pond to refresh the horses. The name of this hamlet is derived from William de Valance, Earl of Pembroke, who was granted the manor in 1249. By this time there was already a church and the large yew in the church yard was already two hundred years old. The current church was largely rebuilt in the 19th century and amongst its treasures is a beautiful 13th century piscina. Gilbert White touched Newton Valance also, for he was curate here between 1755 and 1757.*

To continue our route however, turn left to, after approximately twenty paces, meet a crossing track and a footpath sign indicating the church path back to Selborne. Here you should turn right to follow a track signposted as a bridleway. The track takes you downhill and almost immediately bends left.

Continuing downhill the track follows the line of some fields to your right and then sometime later, the woodland gives way altogether and you will find yourself following the track between fields. Eventually you will come to a lane which you should cross to pass through a small wooden gate the other side into a field. Go diagonally left across the field to the far left hand corner where it is worth stopping awhile to take in the view behind you.

On leaving the field, you will meet another lane on to which you should turn right and follow for approximately twenty paces. Here the lane bends left, but you should leave it to continue straight on along a marked bridleway which runs gently uphill through a small wood, Bridleway Copse. It soon emerges however, to continue between fields with views to your left of "Charity Farm" and beyond it the hill we will shortly have to climb, Noar Hill.

The bridleway leads to the drive to "Charity Farm" which you should cross to continue ahead, now following the left hand perimeter of a field. Continue along the left hand perimeter to skirt woodland and stay following the field perimeter until you eventually meet a stile on your left, just before the field ends. Cross the stile to enter the start of the woodland covering Noar Hill. You will now follow a fairly narrow path where after a short distance, you will join another path coming in from the right to continue ahead. Soon after, the path forks and you should ignore the left fork to continue straight on for a few paces. Here you should ignore a path off to the right and another immediately after off to the left, to still continue ahead. Approximately ten paces on you should ignore a second path right signposted as the Hanger Way.

The path you are on now follows a narrow strip of woodland around the steep side of Noar Hill appropriately called Noar Hill Hanger. Occasionally, there are gaps in the trees affording excellent views right to Weathem Hill and the beautifully named Shoulder of Mutton Hill which overlooks Petersfield. Continue your route for some distance around the side of the hill, ignoring sometime later, a path off to the left marked by a black arrow. The path you are on now begins a gradual descent down the side of Noar Hill, where on nearing the bottom just before the trees give way to fields, you should take a minor path (a bridleway) left. If you find yourself beside a gate at a field, then you have gone too far and should retrace your steps.

The bridleway winds through woodland skirting the base of another hanger, High Wood Hanger. You should ignore all minor paths off to the left or right and also a marked footpath right. As you continue, there are excellent views right across the fields to Selborne. The path eventually begins to climb uphill widening as it goes. Near the top of the hill, it meets a signposted footpath on the right (OS. 743321). Take this, crossing a stile into a field, where you are immediately rewarded with excellent views again across to Selborne. Follow the footpath along the left hand perimeter of the field and at the far side, cross a stile into the next field.

Go diagonally right across the field to reach the corner of the hedgerow ahead. On meeting the hedgerow, cross a stile into another field and follow the right hand perimeter ahead. Two thirds of the way across the field, turn right through a gap in the hedge in the direction of the footpath sign. Go straight across the corner of the next field and on meeting another footpath sign, continue ahead, bearing left to follow the left hand perimeter of the field.

Stay on the path as it leaves the field and continue ahead through a newly planted coppice. This leads to a road, the B3006. Cross over a stile and turn left to pass a small fountain in memory of Gilbert White. The fountain is victorian and is in the form of a lion's mouth from which spring water gushes. Up until the early part of this century it was the main supply of water to Selborne. Immediately after, cross the road and join a concrete drive signposted as a footpath the other side. This passes between cottages and then through a gate, after which you should continue straight on to meet a field. At the field turn left to follow the left hand perimeter in the direction of the footpath sign. At the corner of the field turn right to continue along the left hand perimeter, where as you progress you will enjoy increasingly good views right back to Noar Hill.

Again, on reaching the field corner, continue round still following the left hand perimeter, where on your left through the trees there is an orchard. On meeting a track on your left, take this following the orchard perimeter to meet a lane. Turn left along the lane and follow this for a short distance until you meet a large stone building on the left, "Sotherington Farm". Turn left here to join an old track to the left of the building, which is lined by shallow banks covered with holly and beech trees. In summer with the canopy thick above your head, it can feel very much like walking through a tunnel. On your right where gaps allow, you will see a large orchard. On the left in the distance is Selborne Common.

Follow the track as it later crosses over another track joining fields and follow it to eventually lead out to a lane, known as Honey Lane. Immediately in front of you at this point, you will have a magnificent view over the Royal Aerospace station and its strange golf ball like radar. Below you in the valley, Oakhanger Valley, is a lovely old farmhouse originally the site of Selborne Priory and now aptly named "Priory Farm". Turn right along the lane until you meet a small road off to the left marked as a dead end. Do not take this road, but leave the lane to cross a stile ahead into a field marked by a yellow arrow as a footpath.

Go straight ahead and cross the centre of the field to meet and cross a stile at the far side and continue straight on across the next field, following the left hand perimeter downhill. Cross a stile at the end of the field and continue your route following the left hand perimeter of the next field. You are now in the Oakhanger Valley proper.

As the field perimeter bends left you should leave it to continue straight on, now crossing the centre of the field heading for a stile in the hedgerow ahead. Cross the stile, a dual stile, and carry straight on along the right hand perimeter of a field and at the far side pass through a gate on to a track where you should turn left. Follow the track as it bends round to the right and just after, bear left over a stile into a field. Go diagonally right across the field to reach and cross another stile. Cross the next field, ignoring a stile on your left, to go over a third stile ahead at the far side.

Cross the next field to reach the left hand perimeter and then follow this until you meet a junction of footpaths which are signposted. Here you should turn left along a muddy track leading you away from the field over the Oakhanger stream.

i   **The Oakhanger Stream and Chapel Farm.** *This beautiful little stream starts from a series of springs below Selborne Hanger. Most of the springs are intermittent, only flowing in wet weather. The name for such a spring is a bourne and explains the "bourne" found in many village names, including Selborne. From here, the Oakhanger stream rapidly gathers strength to eventually flow into the river Wey. Across the fields, is Chapel Farm and beside it a field known as Chapel Field. The farm is named after a chapel of ease which was part of Selborne Priory and the adjacent field is believed to be the site of the chapel. Gilbert White searched extensively for traces of the chapel, though all he found was a large hollow stone which could have been the chapel's font. The farmer at the time was unceremoniously using it as a trough for his pigs!*

Immediately after crossing the stream you should turn right, thereby leaving the track to follow the stream and the right hand perimeter of a field. At the corner of the field cross over a stile and two small wooden plank bridges and continue ahead across the next field bearing slightly right. The Royal Aerospace station is now very close with the golf ball constructions looming just ahead of you.

At the far right hand corner of the field, turn right to cross a small wooden plank bridge and then a stile into the next field. Turn immediately left and follow the left hand perimeter of the field round until you meet a stile over which you should pass, to arrive at a road beside a thatched cottage. Cross the road, turn left and follow the road passing the entrance on your left to the aerospace station to enter the village of Oakhanger. Sometime after on your left, you will meet "The Red Lion" pub, a friendly Courage pub which serves food and a good half way stop.

Continue along the road after the pub ignoring a footpath off to your right. After a short distance you will arrive at Shortheath which is a continuation of Oakhanger, with its chapel on the left and on your right the village hall with its unusual porch. Shortheath also has a common which if you have time, is a pleasant place to explore.

Pass the small village green and continue along the road until you meet a second smaller chapel on your left, with two stones in the wall recording its errection by public subscription in 1820 and its enlargement in 1850. Immediately after the chapel, turn left along a track which is signposted as a public footpath and pass the chapel. Thereafter, the track runs between houses before leaving Shortheath to run between fields. To your left the aerospace station is still visible.

The track later bends right and then left to pass "Binswood Farm" (OS. 766367). As the track bends left again to enter the farmyard itself, you should leave it to turn right over a stile beside a wooden gate. You are now joining a marked footpath to enter Binswood itself, owned by the Woodland Trust. Follow the footpath through the woodland, a beautiful walk particularly in summer and an area with real similarities with parts of the New Forest. The path runs in a straight line through an untouched area of mixed woodland and open grassland. As a guide, there are yellow dots on the tree trunks from time to time, indicating you are still following a public footpath.

Eventually the path meets another signposted footpath in front of a wooden plank bridge and stile (OS. 759371). The view ahead at this point, slightly to your left, is of King John's Hill. You should ignore the bridge and stile and turn left to go almost back on yourself away from the stile. You are now following the Hanger Way marked as a public footpath by yellow markings and also as the Hanger Way by way of black arrows on a white background. After approximately twenty metres, the path forks and you should take the left and more prominent path, following the yellow markings and black arrows. After a few paces, this joins a path coming in from the left to continue straight on. It again becomes more prominent as you progress and later forks. Here you should take the right hand fork following a line of bushes on your right.

Oak

Shortly after, you will meet a signposted footpath on the right, again marked by the black arrow, which you should take. You will soon meet another footpath sign, this time pointing left and again you should follow this crossing over a small wooden bridge and stay on the path as it continues through woodland. The route is marked in places with the yellow footpath signs and the black arrows of the Hanger Way.

After a short distance, the path leads out onto a wider grass track where you should bear left, again following the footpath signs. This leads to a stile at the edge of a field which you should cross. Go diagonally right across the field heading for the far corner where you should cross another stile to continue straight on, once more through woodland. Look out for a footpath sign on your left which you should take to follow a narrow footpath for a short while, which leads out to a small pond surrounded by bull rushes.

Follow the footpath as it skirts the left hand bank of the pond to continue, once round the pond, back into woodland. On meeting a prominent track, turn left still in the direction of the footpath signs and after approximately forty metres turn right onto another marked track. This leads gently uphill and at the top bends round to the left. Here you should ignore a less defined track off to the right to continue uphill and later ignore another track off to the left. The track eventually levels out and then bends right to meet a lane beside a large house with its own small lake.

Turn right along the lane, taking time to stop at a farm gate on the right to look back and admire the view and after approximately fifty metres turn left along another lane signposted to Candover. This is still part of the Hanger Way. A short detour before turning left is available to the church of Hartley Mauditt with its deserted village. To do this you should stay on the lane, i.e. not turning left to Candover and continue uphill where the lane joins a footpath leading straight to the church (the distance there and back is two miles).

Our route however, is left in the direction of Candover. You will pass a number of lovely cottages on your left where the lane gives way to a track. After passing a converted barn, "Candover Barn", you should ignore a signposted footpath off to the left and follow the track which goes gently uphill. The track ends at a field gate where you should take the signposted footpath to the right of it which runs above the field. Be warned, the next part of the walk can be extremely muddy in wet weather. To compensate, there are superb views left across to Bordon Camp, the spire of Blackmore church and Woolmer Forest. Sometime later, you will meet a signposted footpath on the right which as before, you should ignore to continue ahead.

The field on your left soon ends and the path, now a track, continues through Wick Wood for some distance, until you eventually meet a field on your right and a stile beside a metal gate. You should ignore these to carry straight on, thereby leaving the Hanger Way, until you meet two stiles, one either side of the track. This is also where the tree line breaks, the farm directly ahead of you is "Priory Farm". The priory itself was unusually closed by the Bishop of Winchester who learned that the priory was involved in activities of a dubious nature.

Go over the stile on your right and continue ahead along the right hand perimeter of a field. At the bottom of the valley on your left is the Oakhanger stream and above it, you can just trace the earlier part of our walk. At the far side of the field, cross a stile to join a narrow path and continue ahead through woodland to meet and cross another stile into a field. Cross the field ahead, bearing gently right, to reach the far corner. The field can at times be very wet and there are wooden plank bridges to assist your route.

At the far corner of the field cross over a stile and join a wide path which continues ahead through woodland. The Oakhanger stream is still following your route on the left, where there is soon a thick line of poplar trees giving a very french feel to the surroundings. Stay on the footpath to meet at the end of the woodland, a National Trust sign informing you that you have just been traversing an area known as the Long Lythe. The path then crosses a short piece of open field before passing between wooden posts to follow a beautiful strip of beech woodland, the Short Lythe. As you progress, you should ignore a footpath off to the left and continue ahead to pass a lovely old cottage on the left before crossing a tributary of the Oakhanger stream, Seale stream, into a field. Go straight across the field, now going sharply uphill, with the stream meandering perfectly off to the right. As you continue up the hill, known as Church Meadow, the Glebe Field, St. Mary's church will come into view.

St. Mary's, Selborne (OS. 741338 Map 186) is a pleasant way to enter Selborne, though it means we discover Gilbert White in reverse for it is here that he was laid to rest. The gravestone is to be found on the north side of the chancel and is inscribed simply "G.W. - 26th June, 1793". Outside the entrance to the church are the remains of the Selborne yew. I say remains for the yew was blown down in a storm on 25th January, 1990. Tangled in its exposed roots were several human bones and broken pottery dating back to 1200 AD. The great yew, over one thousand fourhundred years old, was in its life time studied and admired by both Gilbert White and William Cobbett. The tree has been replanted in the hope that it will recover but the early signs are not promising.

The church itself is a grand affair, it is in the main Norman immediately recognisable by its majestic arches. In the floor of the chancel is a large black stone commemorating

Gilbert White's grandfather and vicar of this church between 1681 and 1728.

Walk through the church yard exit to arrive at a small green. This is known as The Plestor and is an attractive place to just sit and watch the world go by. The name is derived from Play Stow which means "play area". It was here that much of the village's festivities took place and Gilbert White remembers it as a place where the villagers liked to gather to pass their free time. From The Plestor walk to the road, the B3006 and turn left to walk through the village of Selborne.

Selborne Church

Selborne (OS. 742337 Map 186) *is much as Gilbert White would have remembered it. His home, "The Wakes" (now a museum), is still opposite the old butcher's shop and the limes he planted to hide its front still grow. Just up from the butcher's shop is the inn he favoured, still serving a decent pint of ale and offering a place to stay to road-weary travellers. "The Wakes" is most peoples' first stop when visiting Selborne. The house in which White spent his later years is a fitting tribute to the man, particularly the garden which was originally the inspiration for his work and still much as he left it.*

The house itself was built around 1500 when it was but a small cottage. The house came into the White family when Gilbert White's grandfather purchased it in the early 1700's. Gilbert White inherited it in 1763. The house is also a museum and tribute to the explorers Frank and Lawrence Oates. It is an endowment from another member of the Oates family, Robert Oates, which enabled the museum to be set up. For details of opening hours telephone: 042050 275.

Apart from "The Wakes", Selborne also has a Romany museum specialising in english folklore. There are also a number of souvenir and gift shops as well as a book shop. For refreshments, there is "The Queens Hotel", Courage and "The Selborne Arms", Courage. Both serve food. A tea shop allows refreshments of a non-alcaholic kind and there is a grocer selling a wide range of provisions.

Before you leave, perhaps you can pay your own personal tribute to Gilbert White by promising yourself that the next book you read will be "The Natural History and Antiquities of Selborne".

To arrive back at our starting point, continue through the village to reach "The Selborne Arms" and behind it, the car park.

ACCOMMODATION

The Queens Hotel, Selborne. Tel: 042050 454

On the walk, this is a comfortable refurbished hotel in the heart of Selborne. A nice place to soak up the atmosphere in the evening.

Hurstland, Greatham. Tel: 0420538 369

Two and a half miles from the walk, this is a large, comfortable and relatively modern house with picture windows to show off the view outside to maximum effect. Rooms are well appointed with everything you need for a pleasant stay.

 Youth Hostel, Hindhead YHA, Hindhead. Tel: 0428 734285

 Approximately eleven miles from the walk, a simple youth hostel situated in the bowl of the Devil's Punchbowl. Basic but idyllic, I loved it. Camping is also permitted.

 Camping and Carvanning, Tilford Touring, Tilford. Tel: 025125 3296

Approximately fifteen miles from the walk, this site is in a particularly nice setting surrounded by Hankley Common, within walking distance of "The Duke of Cambridge" pub. The site is open all year.

DESERT RUN

Distance: 12¾ miles (20·5 km)

Time: Allow approximately 7 hours, more if you visit Whitsbury

Map: Ordnance Survey Landranger Map 184

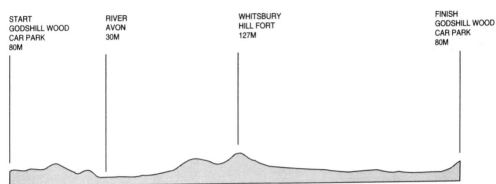

START	RIVER	WHITSBURY	FINISH
GODSHILL WOOD	AVON	HILL FORT	GODSHILL WOOD
CAR PARK	30M	127M	CAR PARK
80M			80M

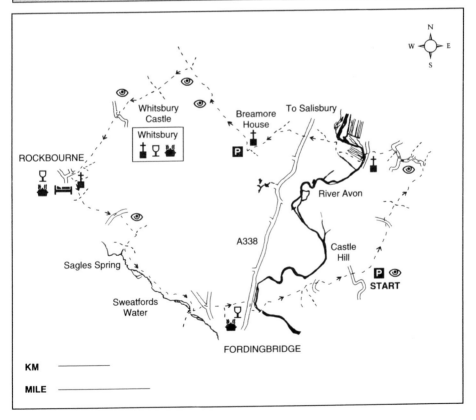

Walk Summary

Desert Run explores the contrasting high ground either side of the Hampshire Avon. From the New Forest you cross the Avon to encounter wide fields dissected by ancient tracks, scenery typical of nearby Wiltshire. You will also pass through some idyllic villages with equally idyllic pubs, so make sure you allow plenty of time. There are no extreme gradients, the ascents are gradual but can be long and therefore surprisingly tiring.

Start - OS. 177161 Map 184

The walk starts from Godshill Wood car park. To get there from Fordingbridge take the B3078 east to Godshill. On reaching Godshill, turn left at The Fighting Cocks Inn to take a lane signposted to Woodgreen. Go over a ford (known locally as the Splash) after which ignore a turning off to the left and continue uphill until the lane bends sharp left. Here you should turn right into the car park. If you are coming from the east, take the M27 and at junction 1, turn north onto the B3079. At Brook take the B3078 signposted to Fordingbridge and stay on it until you reach Godshill. At Godshill, turn right immediately after The Fighting Cocks Inn and follow the directions given above to reach Godshill Wood car park. There is no obvious alternative start point.

DESERT RUN

At the car park, you are immediately without any effort rewarded with lovely views across to Godshill Ridge. The car park is in itself a beauty spot and in summer, well used as an all day picnic area.

Walk to the end of the car park, heading north, to pass through a small wooden gate on the left adjacent to a one bar gate. Turn left after the gate and follow the path ahead through the wood which can be muddy, to reach a gravel track on to which you should turn right. Follow the gravel track ignoring all turnings off passing through a pleasant mixture of conifers and deciduous woodland.

The track later becomes somewhat less defined before eventually arriving at "Godshill Wood Cottage" (OS. 181173). Here you should pass through a wooden gate to reach and cross a lane ahead. Join a gravel track the other side signposted to "Neterhat" and ignore a drive off to the left which leads into a property, "Hill Down". Continue on the track, now signposted as a footpath and pass over a cattle grid. Immediately after the cattle grid the path forks and you should take the right hand fork, the left hand leads directly to "Neterhat". The footpath is now signposted to "North Densome" and continues curving round to the left. Just before "North Densome" look out for a narrow footpath on the right which is marked by a yellow arrow. This is fenced and leads downhill along the perimeter of "North Densome" on your left with beech and holly woods on the right.

Follow the path and cross a small stream via a narrow plank bridge and after a short distance, cross a second stream. On meeting a stile, cross this into a field and continue ahead along the left hand perimeter to cross another stile at the far side. Go straight across the next field, which in summer is a mass of wild flowers and grasses and cross a third stile to reach a "T" junction. Turn right and after approximately thirty paces, left on to a track signposted as a bridleway. This leads downhill and passes a lovely cottage on the left complete with swimming pool.

Shortly after the cottage the track forks and you should follow the right hand fork, signposted as a bridleway, to go uphill. This leads up through an area of rhododendron bushes and holly, known as Stricklands Plantation and is particularly pretty in late spring and early summer. It later breaks away from the rhododendrons to arrive at a clearing and passes under a large electricity pilon before re-entering woodland and undergrowth. On a clear day to your left at the clearing, you may be lucky enough to catch a glimpse of "Breamore House" which we will pass later on our walk. Stay on the track, now more a path, as it continues through very beautiful and well established sweet chestnuts which act as a host to many well fed squirrels, until you meet a narrow but well defined crossing path on to which you should turn left. If you look right at this point, the appearance is of a tunnel leading uphill.

Follow the path which now goes downhill to reach the bottom of a valley. Here you should meet and cross a small stream to continue up the other side, gradually leaving the woodland to follow a fenced path between fields. On nearing the top, pass through a metal gate and continue straight on to reach a gravel drive. Carry straight on as the gravel drive becomes tarmac and ignore another drive and then a footpath on your right. Follow the drive, now a lane, to pass a number of lovely properties on the left, one in particular being "The Old Rectory". The lane ends beside "Garden Cottage" which has a post box in its wall. Here you should turn right onto another lane going uphill, where as the hedge breaks in places there are excellent views to your left over the Avon valley.

As you progress, ignore a signposted footpath on your left to Woodgreen and continue, passing the main entrance and gatehouse to "Hale Park".

Hale Park (OS. 180186 Map 184). The house as we see it today, was designed and built by one Thomas Archer who bought the estate in 1715. He was a famous architect of his time and Queen Anne commissioned him to build several churches in London. As we later pass close to the house, you will understand his popularity. Since 1715, there have been several alterations but the original clock tower still remains. The main drive, now broken by the lane on which we have been

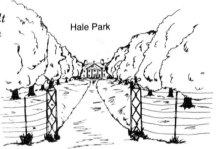

Hale Park

walking, is a mile long and ends at Hatchet Green. The lodge at the beginning of the drive at Hatchet Green is a copy of one at Hyde Park. The avenue of lime trees along the drive are said to have been planted by Thomas Archer himself.

Immediately after the entrance to "Hale Park", look out for a footpath on your left signposted as the Avon Valley Path and also "Footpath to Church". Take this path, which runs parallel to the main drive and follow it as it crosses over a gravel drive sometime later. Continue straight on to pass close to the right of the property and then follow the path as it bends right. Do not join the track on your left but continue on the narrow path beside it. Pass through an old iron gate into woodland going downhill, following a somewhat hidden stream on your right. This will soon bring you to the church of St. Mary's, a lovely spot with excellent views behind it of "Hale Park".

The Church of St. Mary (OS. 178187 Map 184). The church to the manor was built in 1631 on the site of a 14th century church. It was altered greatly in 1717 by Thomas Archer to its present style. On the floor of the church is a magnificent heraldic brass dedicated to Sir John Peniuddocke, who held Hale Park in the 16th century. The most striking monument in the church is the huge marble statue of Thomas Archer himself.

After the church, follow the narrow path downhill to pass through a kissing gate on to a small lane. Cross the lane and carry straight on along a track signposted as a right of way, to cross a concrete bridge over the river Avon.

i *The Battle of Charford (OS. 175186 Map 184). The landscape around you is tranquility itself and it is hard not to feel you are intruding. Yet centuries ago in 519 AD, this part of the Avon known as Charford was the site of a bloody battle, arguably the start of the Saxon kingdom of Wessex.*

It was Cerdica, a Saxon chiefton and his son Cynric, who sailed up the river Avon to this point to confront the tribal ancient Britons who had regrouped following the departure of the Romans and had their stronghold at Old Sarum. The Saxons won the day but such was the ferocity of the battle, that they made no attempt to advance and take Old Sarum. Instead, they chose to stop and consolidate their stronghold on the area already conquered. For fourteen years, Cerdica stayed head of his small kingdom, too nervous to attack the famous hill forts of Hampshire and Wiltshire. After this, he moved north leaving the tiny kingdom he had created to his son Cynric. It took Cynric another thirtytwo years before he eventually captured Old Sarum and so tentatively started the kingdom of Wessex.

There followed an unsettling period, now known as the Dark Ages, from which many legends have grown. It was not until three centuries later that the Saxon kings gained full law and order and mapped out proper the kingdom of Wessex. The rest is history, well recorded, but few people today realise the important role played by this tranquil part of the Avon valley.

Pass through a gate at the other side of the bridge and turn left across a field following the river on your left, to shortly pass over a small wooden bridge and then through another gate into the next field. Go straight across the field and head for the farm gate ahead passing over another small wooden bridge. Do not pass through the farm gate, but turn right just before it and continue along the left hand perimeter of the field walking away from the river Avon.

At the far corner cross over a stile on your left and go over a narrow footbridge into a field, where you should continue along the right hand perimeter. Follow the field perimeter until you meet a small sometimes hidden footbridge on your right, which you should cross to follow a narrow path ahead. On meeting a stile, cross this into a field and go straight across the field cutting across the left hand corner. Ahead to your right now is "South Charford Farm", our next destination and beyond to the left, "Breamore House".

Go over another narrow footbridge beside the remains of some old sluice gates and turn right on to a wide farm track. The track bends round to the right where as you progress, you will gain good views to your right back to "Hale Park" and St. Mary's church. It then bends left towards the farm and you should follow it to arrive at the farm yard, with the farmhouse on your left and the yard itself on the right. Do not turn right, but carry straight on between the farm buildings to pass through a metal farm gate and continue ahead along a farm track. As the track bends left, leave it to continue straight on and enter a field immediately ahead. Go straight across the field heading for a stile at the far side, just to the right of a thatched cottage.

Cross the stile and continue straight on to cross a second stile into a field. Go straight across the field and at the far side, cross over a wooden footbridge and then a stile to arrive at a layby beside the A338, the main road between Salisbury and Bournemouth.

Continue ahead to cross the main road and thereafter, a stile into a field. Cross the field in the direction of the footpath sign and at the far side, go over a stile to carry straight on across the next field heading for a copse. At the copse, cross a stile and turn left to follow a narrow footpath gently uphill which can in summer be somewhat overgrown and protective clothing may therefore, be necessary.

Stay on the footpath passing through the copse to reach a field beside a stile and farm gate. Ahead to your right now is "Breamore House". Go over the stile and follow the right hand perimeter of a field. Do not be tempted to follow the track which later bends left. At the far side of the field, cross a stile and continue straight across the next field in the direction of the yellow arrow, heading for the right hand corner. At the corner pass through a metal gate and continue, going diagonally left, across a field heading for a stile just to the right of a small house, somewhat hidden by trees. The stile, as a guide, is almost half way between "Breamore House" on your right and the smaller house visible on your left.

Go over the stile which leads you straight into the church yard of Breamore Parish Church.

Breamore Church (OS. 153189 Map 184). *This famous Saxon church is over one thousand years old, being built during the reign of King Cnute. The one remaining Saxon arch in the tower has some of the oldest carved words in England. They read "Here the covenant becomes manifest to thee".*

Follow the path to the church door and after perhaps visiting the church, turn left and leave the church yard by the main path which leads to a small parking area. Continue on to meet the main drive and entrance to "Breamore House" on to which you should turn right. On your left here is a sign for a museum and tea room. Pass through the entrance, guarded by lions and follow the drive as it sweeps to the left of the house.

Breamore House (OS. 152191 Map 184). *This is the closest you will come to the house unless you actually visit it, though the owners may not take kindly to your muddy walking boots! From here though, you can be content to admire the magnificent Elizabethan architecture. The house was built in 1583 by Queen Elizabeth's Treasurer, William Doddington. In 1748, the Hulse family became owners of the house and have kept it to the present day. The house is now open to the public during the summer and attached, is an interesting countryside and carriage museum. Jousting tournaments are also held in the grounds. The house is said to be haunted by several ghosts so ensure you pass this way with plenty of time to spare before dark!*

Continue uphill passing the stables, where the drive becomes a gravel track and enters Breamore Wood. Stay on the track through the woods ignoring any tracks or paths off to the left or right. After approximately three quarters of a mile, the track suddenly leaves the wood and you immediately gain excellent views to your left of "Down Farm" and across a sweeping valley to "Manor Farm" at Whitsbury. Continuing, the track meets a "T" junction where you should turn left (the track right is private), thereby keeping to the main track which now runs between hedges. You will soon arrive at open hillside where three tracks fan out in front of you. You must take the centre track which goes uphill heading for trees and a white sign ahead pointing left to the Miz Maze. This hill is a lovely place to stop for a picnic, particularly in summer when it is full of summer flowers and grasses and frequented by numerous varieties of butterfly. The crest of the hill is wooded and a narrow path entering the wood leads you to the Miz Maze.

i **The Miz Maze (OS. 142202 Map 184)** *is a chalk and turf circular maze, a style of maze unique to England. This one is one of the best preserved in the country. Its origin and purpose is uncertain. Many believe that the maze is of neolithic origin, a theory backed up by the numerous traces of their activity in the immediate vacinity. In particular, Clearbury Ring and Whitsbury Camp, the latter of which we soon pass and further away, the revered capital of these people, Old Sarum.*

Another theory is that it was a monastic creation, built by the monks of the old priory at Breamore. Mazes often played an important part in religion during the Middle Ages and on the Continent were often incorporated in the tiled floors of churches.

There are several theories as to their purpose, one of the most common is that the maze represents the maze of life. Others believe it was used for a dance pattern or as a form of penance. Monks are said to have been made to crawl on their hands and knees to the centre and locals tell that a man can run to Gallows Hill and back, a journey of just over a mile, before a man can crawl to the centre. One of the strongest theories and one associated with many legends, is that the maze is the key to afterlife and crawling along it without making a mistake will take you there. Just in case it's true I suggest you don't try it!

To continue our route, pass the sign for the Miz Maze and follow the tree line round the top of the hill to descend the other side bearing gently right. At the bottom the path joins another track on to which you should turn left, to continue with fencing on your left and hedgerow on the right. Shortly after, you will meet a stile and track going off to the left, marked by a yellow arrow. Turn left over the stile and continue ahead along the left hand perimeter of a field, where on your right another group of trees mark the site of an old round barrow.

At the far side of the field, continue straight on entering woodland where shortly you will meet a crossing track beside a barn on your right. Go straight over the crossing track and continue along a grass path which soon leads out into a field. Here you should follow the left hand perimeter to the far side of the field where you should go over a stile beside a metal gate. Thereafter, go straight on over two crossing tracks to join a track ahead which is fenced on your right and hedged on the left. The track leads uphill and is something of a long climb, but you are rewarded as you progress with increasingly good views.

As you reach the top of the hill "Manor Farm" reappears. At the same time you are rewarded with magnificent views to the north west and a close look at your map will confirm that apart from Hampshire, you are also admiring the countryside of Dorset and Wiltshire. To the north, Clearbury hill fort better known as Clearbury Ring, is clearly recognisable. On a clear day and slightly to its left in the distance, the slender spire of Salisbury cathedral is visible. The view was not missed by our ancestors as behind you, hidden among the trees, are the remains of another iron age hill fort, Whitsbury Castle.

i **Whitsbury Castle (OS. 128197 Map 184)** *was the largest in a long line of forts defending the west bank of the Avon. A similar line of forts defended the eastern bank and together, they halted Cerdica's advance into Celtic Briton. The fort's defences included three banks, the inner one nearly twentytwo feet in height being the second highest in Hampshire. During its life, the fort was used by the Romans who sank a three hundred foot well at its western entrance.*

After admiring the view and catching your breath, continue along the track to pass through a metal farm gate, after which you should ignore a track off to the right to carry straight on. The track then bends left to join a tarmac drive where a large white manor house comes into view. You should turn immediately right and pass to the right of a large brick and timber barn and then left in front of the barn which is in fact stables. Follow the drive between white fences to reach a lane beside the entrance on your left to the manor, "Whitsbury Manor Stud", owned for some years by the bookmaker William Hill of horse racing fame. In summer you may be lucky, as on certain days the gardens are open for teas.

Should you wish to visit the main village of Whitsbury, then turn left at the lane.

Whitsbury (OS. 128190 Map 184) is one of many picture postcard villages that nestle in the Western Downlands. A good way to explore the village, is to take a track signposted "To the Church" from Whitsbury Manor Stud and then from the church take the steep path down to the village centre. From the village centre you can complete a small circle by returning to Whitsbury Manor Stud via the lane.

The first stop on this itinerary is the village church of St. Leonard. This occupies a hill top position with views from the church yard across the Avon to the New Forest. The unusual brick church of today, was largely built in the early 19th century on the site of an earlier church. From the church tower there descends a path to the village and from this, there are pleasant views across a field to a large house. In years gone by an annual hog fair was held in the field.

The main attraction of the village apart from its charming cottages, is The Cart Wheel, the village pub. This is a free house and aside of an exhaustive range of real ale, serves up an original and carefully prepared menu. Unlike so many other country pubs, The Cart Wheel has not forgotten the local population and an evening or even a lunchtime here, can be a lively affair.

Returning via the lane you will pass a large house with more stables. Outside the house are two sarson stones, their original purpose being uncertain, though it is likely they were once part of a circle or dolmen. With such a lot of the village dedicated to horse racing, it is not surprising that apart from William Hill the village is associated with another equally well known and respected name from the sport. This is Desert Orchid, probably the most famous of all race horses. Walking back up the lane, especially if you have visited The Cart Wheel, you may just wish that you too had taken up riding instead of walking!

From "Whitsbury Manor Stud", our route continues by turning right along the lane which shortly after, bends right beside two houses. Leave the lane at this point and turn left in front of the two houses along another lane, signposted as a bridleway. This leads past a small green with more houses. Here you should continue straight on and pass through a white gate and follow the drive passing more stables on your left. The drive soon gives way to a grass track almost an avenue, as it is hedged and lined with beech and copper beech trees.

The grass track narrows and then ends at a small iron gate through which you should pass to continue along a fenced path. You will soon meet another small gate beside a larger one. Pass through the small gate to continue straight on, going downhill through a line of mature beech and chestnut trees. When I last walked this route, there was an unusual flock of sheep in the field on the left. This is a particularly lovely part of the walk and leads down to another metal gate and thereafter a larger gate, both of which you should pass through. This takes you into a large open and sweeping field, often grazed by sheep.

Go straight across the field along a grass track heading for the buildings ahead, which are the first signs of Rockbourne village, our next destination. The grass track soon leads you to a tarmac track on to which you should turn right. At the farm buildings, pass through a farm gate and over a cattle grid to follow the drive right passing to the right of the farm and outbuildings. The drive bends left and progresses naturally into a lane and follows the farm wall on your left which is topped by tiles. At the gateway to the farm, you will have lovely views of the manor house and its beautiful old barn. The barn has some well preserved 13th century windows, their design reveals that it was once the chapel for a monastic house, probably run by "Breamore Priory". The farm once belonged to Sir John Cooper, father of the first Earl of Shaftesbury.

At the end of the wall our route is left along a gravel track heading towards the church which is signposted. If however, you wish to visit Rockbourne and its excellent pub, follow the lane to its end.

Rockbourne (OS. 115183 Map 184). The village is almost at once familiar, probably because every year a few of its cottages appear on numerous calendars. It is basically one long street, either side of which are a jumble of period houses and thatched cottages. A stream runs along one side of the road, though the springs that feed it often dry up in summer. As a result of this, the stream is known as a "winterbourne", "bourne" being an ancient word for an intermittent spring. The village pub, The Rose and Thistle, is at the northern end of the village. This excellent free house is another of the many thatched buildings in the village. Inside, you can enjoy a meal in snug surroundings and in the summer, there is a pleasant garden with a thatched dovecot.

Continuing our route, follow the gravel drive to its end, "The Manor House". Just in front of the house, take the second path right behind the yew hedge and ascend a series of gravel steps to the church which is accessed by a gate on your left.

St. Andrews Church (OS. 115184 Map 184) sits on a knoll overlooking the village it serves. Its unusual shape is due to the numerous improvements and alterations over the centuries. The shell of the church is basically 13th century, though there are traces of Norman architecture including a fine arch. Inside the church, one cannot help noticing the many monuments to the Coote family. The most famous member of this family was Sir Eyre Coote, a respected soldier. The village in which Sir Eyre made his home, must have been a welcome refuge after his campaigns in India, of which there were many.

One of Eyre Coote's most famous successes was the attack at Plassey, when with only three thousand men Coote advised Clive to attack an army of fiftyfive thousand. Against all odds, the British won the battle and took command of Bengal. On his death, the British army on Coote's wishes, returned his body to Rockbourne where he is now buried. The East India Company in gratitude to his services, errected a monument in the grounds of his house. This is visible later on the walk.

The decaying flags which still hang in the chancel are a reminder of the British campaigns in India. Their sorry state is due to army etiquette which instructs that a regiments colours can neither be destroyed or preserved.

Pass the church gate on your left and continue along the path which becomes grass for a short distance. Thereafter, you should ignore a signposted footpath off to the left and carry straight on following a brick wall on the right. At the end of the wall, ignore a path off to the right to maintain your course which overlooks the pretty thatched roofs of Rockbourne. As you continue, you should ignore two more footpaths off to the right and carry straight on along the path which now runs behind houses. After the houses you will meet a stile which you should cross, ignoring another footpath at this point off to the right to continue ahead. The path from this point is well defined but you should beware the occasional rabbit hole inviting a twisted or sprained ankle!

The path eventually meets a crossing track where you should go over a stile, across the track and straight ahead over another stile in the direction of the yellow arrows. This path is now hedged and runs between fields and where gaps in the hedges allow, you will see the monument to Sir Eyre Coote on the hill opposite. Soon after, you will meet a field where you should take a well defined path running directly across its centre. At the other side on meeting the line of a wood, you should continue across the field following the perimeter of the wood which acts as the left hand perimeter of the field. As the woodland gives way to the left you should leave it to continue along the path, now going across the field heading for a stile ahead.

Cross the stile to meet a lane on to which you should turn left, going gently uphill. At the brow of the hill leave the lane to take a gravel track right, signposted as a footpath (OS. 125176). You will shortly meet a farm gate and stile which you should cross to continue straight on through woodland, an area of welcome shade on a hot day. The woodland soon breaks where you should ignore a track off to the left, to continue ahead along the track between open fields for some distance. Here, on a clear day you will enjoy magnificent views ahead of the New Forest.

Before the track reaches the tree line, you should leave it to pass through a metal gate on the right, marked as a public footpath. Go straight across a field and at the far side, go over a stile beside another metal gate. Continue ahead along a grass track and as this bends left, leave it to go straight on following the line of the woodland on your right. On meeting the tree line ahead, continue down a very steep bank to meet a junction of tracks. Here you should go straight on, ignoring the tracks off to the left and right.

The track now runs downhill and soon bends left where you should ignore a track going off to the right. It then continues into a field following the right hand perimeter. Here to your right at this point, is a large area of natural habitation. Its lush appearance is due to Sagles Spring, which rises in its midst. The spring is more reliable than those at Rockbourne and forms a pretty stream known as Sweatfords Water which flows into the Avon at Fordingbridge. At the other side of the field, the grass track becomes gravel and soon bends left to reach a metal gate and stile. Go over the stile ignoring a signposted footpath left and continue along the track.

Shortly after the track bends left again where immediately after you should turn right thereby leaving the track, into a field and follow the right hand perimeter. As a guide, there is an old wooden barn on the hill above to your left. At the far side of the field you will see a stile with a yellow arrow. At the time of writing, this was completely overgrown and I found it far easier to follow the grass track, which passes to the left of the stile over a wooden bridge into the next field. After the bridge, continue straight on again following the right hand perimeter of the field. As with many areas on this walk, these fields seem to have been left fallow inviting a mass of wildlife.

At the far side of the field, continue straight on passing through a gap in the hedge into the next field. Follow the right hand perimeter until you reach the far right hand corner. Here you should turn right over a stile to enter woodland and follow a narrow winding path with a small stream, an arm of Sweatfords Water sometimes dry in summer, on your right.

The path leads naturally to another stile on your left which you should cross into a field. Turn right and follow the right hand perimeter of the field, at the far side of which you should join a track just slightly in from the field corner. The track runs through a strip of woodland and enters another field, where you should continue ahead to follow the track as it bends left towards a gateway. Just before the gateway, you should leave the track and turn right on to a path which follows the left hand perimeter of the field. Take care not to miss this.

At the far side of the field the path meets a gate and stile. Cross over the stile and follow a narrow path ahead through more woodland. The path eventually bends right and leads out to a lane beside an electricity sub-station. Turn left along the lane passing to the left of Fordingbridge sub-station to reach another lane in front of some houses where you should turn right (**OS. 143156**). Follow the lane and leave it as it turns right, taking the left turn, signposted to Breamore, called Tinkers Cross and Fryern Court Road. Immediately after joining this road, turn right along a gravel track signposted as a public footpath and to "Newton House".

Continue to pass to the left of "Newton House" and follow the track ahead which runs into the Avon valley, with views in the distance of the New Forest. Ignore a footpath going off to the right and continue ahead along the now signposted Avon Valley Path, marked by a green arrow. To your right and just visible are some of the modern houses of Fordingbridge. After some distance, pass to the left of a white house which was at one time an old railway building, the railway line itself being long since gone. The track arrives at a farm where you should carry straight on to pass "Burgate Farmhouse" on your left, to meet a main road, the A338.

Turn right along the main road, still following the signs for the Avon Valley Path and pass "The Tudor Rose", a 14th century thatched and half timbered freehouse and restaurant and continue until you reach the "Ivy Cottage Tea Room" on your right. At the tea room, cross the main road and join the concrete drive opposite, still marked as the Avon Valley Path and also signposted to "Burgate Manor Farm". Follow the drive straight through the farm looking out for the farmhouse itself on the left which is quite magnificent.

Pass through the farm and after passing the last farm building on your left, turn left along a signposted footpath still in the direction of the Avon Valley Path signs. You should then cross the river Avon by way of a suspension bridge, where it is well worth stopping to admire your surroundings and in particular the small weir to your left. At the other side of the bridge, pass through a small metal gate and continue ahead along a raised bank across the middle of a field. At the far side, go over a smaller concrete bridge and turn right, still following the path.

At the end of the field, pass through a gap in the fence and cross three more small bridges over some of the smaller arms of the river Avon. Thereafter, carry straight on along a fenced track running parallel with one of the arms of the river on your left. As you continue, ignore a track off to the left to go straight on.

After some distance, you will reach a metal gate and stile. Cross over the stile and go straight on to pass over yet another arm of the Avon river where you should ignore a track off to your right. Go over the last of the Avon arms by way of a wide but somewhat rickety bridge and continue ahead, now following for a short while the same arm on your right. This soon leads away from the track off to the right where you finally leave the Avon and its many arms behind.

The track you are on continues straight on and begins to climb gently uphill. Shortly after, ignore a signposted footpath off to the right and continue ahead to pass through "Folds Farm" where you should ignore another footpath off to the right. After the farm, pass over a small stream which runs through a garden on your right and continue on to meet a metal gate and stile. Go over the stile and bear left over small green in the direction of the green arrow. After a short distance, you will meet a gravel track which leads on to a lane. Cross the lane and pass through a small wooden gate adjacent to a larger one ahead, to re-enter the New Forest.

Follow the track ahead which climbs up the side of Castle Hill. On nearing the top, ignore a track going off to the left and continue ahead to soon meet a fork. Take the left hand fork which is the more prominent track and continue straight on, later passing over a crossing track. At this point, as a guide, the majority of the trees are pine. After the crossing track, you should carry straight on through more mixed woodland, ignoring all turnings off until you eventually reach a road. Pass through a gate, cross the road and pass through a gate the other side to continue in the same direction. At the first crossing track, turn right and follow this to retrace your earlier steps back to the car park and our starting point. On a summer's day, if you have any food left and perhaps a bottle of wine you may well wish to join the locals and savour the end of a beautiful day with a picnic and a glass of something - cheers!

ACCOMMODATION

The Compasses Inn, Damerhan. Tel: 07253 231

One and a half miles from the walk, this is a village inn with recently refurbished rooms. The front bar is a popular local meeting place and a pleasant if not exciting environment to spend an evening.

Sheerings, Rockbourne. Tel: 07253 256

A few hundred metres from the walk, this is one of several of Rockbourne's thatched cottages which finds itself as decoration on a calendar. The cottage is everything you would expect inside with low oak beams and inglenook fire places.

Youth Hostel, Salisbury YHA, Salisbury. Tel: 0722 327572

Seven and a half miles from the walk, this is an attractive youth hostel set in two acres of grounds. The only drawback is that it tends to get very full in summer, so book ahead.

Camping and Caravanning, Sandy Balls Estate, Godshill. Tel: 0425 6 53042

Two miles from the walk, this is a New Forest site with every conceivable amenity. It even boasts its own pub.

THE TIN TOWN TREK

Distance: 13¼ miles (21.5 km)
Time: Allow approximately 6½ hours
Map: Ordnance Survey Landranger Map 186

THE TIN TOWN TREK

HAMPSHIRE

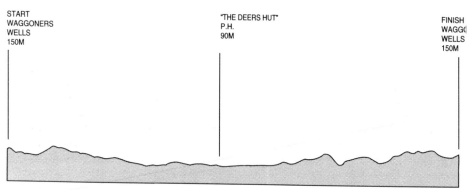

START
WAGGONERS
WELLS
150M

"THE DEERS HUT"
P.H.
90M

FINISH
WAGGO
WELLS
150M

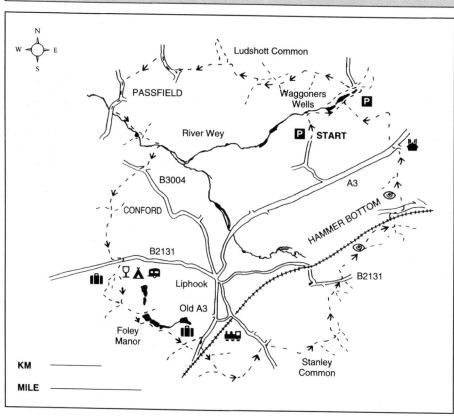

N
W — E
S

Ludshott Common

PASSFIELD

Waggoners
Wells

P

River Wey

P   START

B3004

A3

CONFORD

HAMMER BOTTOM

B2131

B2131

Liphook

Old A3

Foley
Manor

Stanley
Common

KM ——————

MILE ——————

46

Walk Summary

The Tin Town Trek explores one of the least known parts of Hampshire. Much of the route is on military land which, protected from developers, has become a mini-wilderness. Consequently, the countryside through which you pass and especially the woodland, rivals that of any in the south of England. The area is also rich in history and makes the walk one of constant interest. One word of warning, at one point the route crosses the busy A3. If you are taking children or animals, then extra care is required at the point of crossing.

Start - OS. 855337 Map 186

The walk starts from the public car park at Waggoners Wells (National Trust). If coming from the north, take the A3 south until you see the sign for the B2131, Liphook. Take this turning but instead of continuing into Liphook, go right over the A3 and rejoin it, this time on the northbound carriageway. Take the next turning left (currently not signposted so care is needed not to miss it) and follow a lane to its end where there is a parking area. If coming from the south along the A3, take the same turning signposted B2131 (Liphook), but instead of going into Liphook, follow the signs for Bramshott village. On reaching the village church, turn right and follow a narrow lane until you reach a "T" junction. Turn left at the "T" junction and it is a short distance to the car park. If coming by train, there is a station at Liphook. From here it is a short walk south along the old A3 where you can join the route at The Links Hotel. There is no obvious alternative start.

THE TIN TOWN TREK

From the car park at Waggoners Wells take the signposted public footpath which descends through mixed woodland. This follows a fence on your left and in summer is bordered by a mass of foxgloves. Stay on the path to reach the bottom of a valley and continue ahead up a short but steep slope to the top of a small rise. Here you should ignore paths off to the left or right and carry straight on (this could however, be termed as taking the third path off to the right, as almost immediately after joining the path bends right and descends gradually).

Ignore any paths off to the left or right and continue ahead along the side of the rise, where a red brick house will soon come into view on the left just above a small stream. Almost opposite the house, a path joins from the left. You should ignore this to continue straight on passing a "No Horses - No Cyclists" National Trust sign. After a short distance you will arrive at a small lake, one of the Waggoners Wells.

Waggoners Wells (OS. 858342 Map 186), also known as Wakeners Wells, is a series of man-made ponds and one of the sources of the river Wey. The ponds were built by one Henry Hooke to supply power to his iron foundary, unintentionally creating one of the most picturesque beauty spots in Hampshire. You cannot fail to be impressed by Waggoners Wells' immediate charm. The poet, Tennyson, was equally moved when he visited and wrote one of his best known poems "Flower in the Crannied Wall". This refers to flowers growing out of a rough wall of a wishing well which stands beside one of the ponds.

The protection of Waggoners Wells was secured in 1919 when Sir Robert Hunter K.C.B., organised the purchase of the ponds and surrounding land and dedicated it to the public. It is now in the hands of the National Trust. A memorial stone to Sir Robert now stands beside the most northern pond and you can pay your respects when we pass this later en route.

The best time to see the ponds is on an early summer's morning when the mist is rising and the suns ray's dapple the waters inviting the fish to bask under the surface.

Having taken time perhaps to stop and admire the first pond, you should continue to follow the path along the right hand bank which rises gradually. Soon after you will pass an unusual wooden post carved from a tree trunk and then arrive at another of the Waggoners Wells beside a small race. Again, you should continue ahead following the right hand bank of the pond and shortly after, ignore a path going off to the right. This will soon lead you to a third pond also with a small race, where you should go up some steps to continue your route still along the right hand bank. The path will eventually arrive at a small lane and a car park on the right.

At the lane, turn left to cross a ford via a small footbridge and immediately after, turn left to meet a fork. Bear right at the fork to join a signposted public bridleway and go uphill passing the stone memorial to Sir Robert Hunter on the left.

Continue straight on to shortly go over a crossing path and stay on the bridleway as it climbs uphill following the line of an old boundary. At the top of the hill the path levels out to begin the traverse of Ludshott Common, a mixture of open heath and decidious woodland. After some distance, you should ignore a crossing track to continue straight on and thereafter, a minor crossing path to reach a wide track. Cross this to maintain your route straight on where, after a few metres, you will meet another track on to which you should turn left.

The track soon bears right and you are reassured by a sign at this point that you are following a public bridleway. It then follows the perimeter fencing of estate land and later passes two cottages, "Fir Tree" and "Priors". The track ends here but you should continue straight on to pass a wooden post and join a narrow path, a public bridleway. Shortly after, go over a crossing path and continue ahead with fields on your left and the heath on the right. If you have not already realised, the bridleway can be very muddy in wet weather and care is needed.

You will eventually arrive at a gatehouse to Ludshott Estate where you should turn right to follow a footpath leading back onto the common (**OS. 846346**). Ignore a narrow crossing path and continue ahead to meet a "T" junction where you should turn left. You will now follow a line of telegraph poles across the common for approximately a quarter of a mile before the path bears right. Here the path will appear to fork and you should stay on the more prominent path, ignoring the smaller path forking right. The path descends through more dense woodland to reach the bottom of a shallow valley where you will meet a crossing path. Turn left here to follow the bottom of the valley where as a guide, there is a field on your left. The valley is an interesting place and home to just about every species of tree found in the area. When I last walked this way, I was privileged to observe what appeared to be a mating disagreement between three squirrels. The fracas continued for some considerable time and I must say, I was surprised (and impressed) by the persistence of the intruding male.

Stay on the path along the valley bottom and ignore all minor turnings off to eventually meet a bank, part of an old wall on your right. Continue on following the bank to reach and pass a National Trust sign for Gentles Copse. Ignore a path here leading off to the right and carry straight on with fields again on your left and at points, good views across the fields to the wooded hills beyond Liphook. At a fork take the right hand path, continuing straight on to shortly bear round to the right and meet a lane. Here you should continue to bear right to follow the lane, Gentles Lane, passing a large house "High Hurlands" on your left.

After passing another house on the left, "Hurlands", leave the lane taking a path on the left to shortly meet a track. Turn left along the track and continue very gently downhill to later pass between two properties, "The Rock" on your right and "Summerfield" on the left. The track now continues between fields, at one point following a line of poplar trees. You should ignore all turnings off and as you progress, look out for an oast house ahead to your left. In the distance on a clear day you can see the aerial mast on the top of Butser Hill.

The track eventually arrives at a lane, Liphook Road, beside a house named "Tilburys". Turn left along the lane and pass the oast house mentioned earlier, "Passfield House Farm", to enter the village of Passfield with its lovely collection of old English cottages. At a "T" junction, turn right following the signs to Whitehill and Liphook. Pass "The Old Forge" on your right which still has its sun insurance plaque dated 1603. Apart from the normal trade of any forge, this one was unique in that it also manufactured grandfather clocks. The house next door to the forge used to be the village pub, "The Cricketers". Sadly for us this is now closed. Follow the road gently downhill to meet a track on your left signposted as a bridleway. If you find yourself crossing a stream, then you have gone too far along the road and should therefore, retrace your steps. If at this point however, you are in desparate need of liquid refreshments, you can if you wish take the footpath right for a mile detour to reach "The New Robin Hood", a popular free house overlooking a green.

Our route however, joins the bridleway left to pass through a metal farm gate and continues straight on along a wide track which runs above a stream, the river Wey and small lake on your right. The lake is frequented by waterfowl and is part of the Waterside Estate. The track leads to another farm gate beside a red brick house through which you should pass. Continue straight on ignoring bridleways signposted left and right and follow a track ahead with wooden fencing on the right, also signposted as a public bridleway. As you continue, you will gain superb views on your right across the lawns to the main house of "Bramshott Court"(**OS. 832337**). The track leads to a "T" junction in front of a small building owned by Thames Water Authority. Turn right here to shortly pass over the river Wey via a stone bridge and continue along the track to soon begin a gentle climb uphill. You will eventually meet a lane on to which you should turn right to reach a main road, the B3004. Cross the B3004, turn right and after approximately twenty paces, take the signposted public footpath on your left. This path can be slightly overgrown in summer so take care if you are wearing shorts! You are now on Passfield Common which is owned by the National Trust.

Follow the footpath ahead, passing a wooden rail, to run between mixed woodland and bracken. You should ignore a path on your right running almost parallel as this is not a marked footpath. After some distance, pass a second wooden rail to leave the open bracken and continue downhill between holly bushes. This leads down to a small lane where you should turn right in front of a house for approximately ten paces and then left on to a signposted public bridleway. The scattering of houses around you here make up the hamlet of Conford.

After approximately twentyfive metres turn right, still following the public bridleway signs, to lead out behind the houses and the local school to a small green which belongs to the National Trust. Bear left here away from the hamlet to meet a more prominent path on to which you should turn left. This path, a bridleway, now takes you through some beautiful woodland and shortly passes over a stream via a concrete bridge, an area often alive in summer with dragon flies. After the bridge, the path begins to climb uphill later passing two red brick houses on the left and then re-enters woodland to shortly meet a narrow lane. Cross the lane and continue straight on in the direction of the public bridleway sign. Do not take the path, a public footpath, on the left. Take head also, of any "Out of Bounds" signs in this area, as these denote the perimeter of army land and the possibility of unexploded shells!

The bridleway which is fairly prominent continues through mature woodland, Woolmer Forest. Ignore a footpath joining from the left to continue straight on, still going gently uphill. At the top of the hill the path will arrive at the busy A3, the new bypass around Liphook. Turn left here to cross the A3 via a footbridge and at the other side, turn right to follow the A3 for a short distance until you meet a marked public bridleway on the left. Do not make the mistake of joining the wide track just after the bridleway, this again is army land and out of bounds.

i   **The Holly Water Loop** *The wide track just beyond the bridleway is the old course of a private railway known as The Holly Water Loop. It was used by the army to train the Royal Engineers on the construction and operation of a railway. The railway ran from Bordon Camp to Longmoor Camp with the Loop skirting Woolmer Forest, once a royal hunting forest. The railway, as you can see, is long gone though Woolmer Forest is still very much part of the military which has three firing ranges in its depths, a good reason to keep to the bridleway.*

Follow the bridleway away from the A3 downhill through more attractive woodland with a carpet of grasses and stay on it as it later bends left in front of a road, the B2131. Continue with the road running parallel on your right, where shortly through the trees you will see the sign for "Kosaido Old Thorns", a hotel with restaurant and golf course. Stay on the bridleway still following the road and take care not to follow a path left which takes you back into Woolmer Forest. You will eventually bear right to join the B2131 beside a red brick house. Cross the road here, turn left and after approximately twenty metres, turn right on to a path signposted as a right of way. This leads you almost back on yourself and soon arrives at "The Deershut", a Courage pub with a small camp site.

Continue ahead along the drive passing the pub on your left and where the green ends, take a gravel drive off to the left and follow this as it bends right, passing the last of the houses on your left. After the last cottage, "Woodland View", carry straight on along a smaller track signposted as a bridleway, to continue through woodland known as Holly Hills. You should ignore turnings off to the left or right and stay on the track later passing more properties on your left, to wind through the woodland and eventually arrive at two tile hung houses on your left and a more prominent track. Ignore two bridleways off to the right here and follow the track ahead which progresses into a narrow tarmac drive to run between fields. A clock tower immediately comes into view at the top of the hill ahead to your right. This belongs to "Foley Manor".

After a short distance, pass a cottage on your left with a walled garden and thereafter, a small orchard. The drive now winds uphill to reach a "T" junction where the turning right leads to the estate office and "Foley Farm". Our route is left at the "T" junction along the drive to run downhill with the walled garden on your left and shortly after, two small but beautiful lakes. The lakes are quite unexpected. Beautifully landscaped and obviously well cared for, they are at the same time, untouched and forgotten and you cannot help feeling that you have stumbled on somebody's secret. Stay on the drive which is lined by a mass of rhododendron bushes and pass between two stone gate posts to arrive at an enormous statue of Field Marshal Hugh Rose, Lord Strathnairn, astride his horse. The statue guards the main entrance to "Foley Manor" and faces another stunning lake which in mid-summer, is covered with lillies in full bloom.

Field Marshal Hugh Rose, as the inscription informs you, was Commander in Chief of India from 1861 to 1865. At the time of his posting, the Indians were rebelling against the British, with many of the Indian regiments mutinying to join their fellow countrymen against the British army.

Sir Hugh Rose along with Sir Colin Campbell were in the main, responsible for the rebels eventual defeat. This came about in a series of well organised but brutal campaigns which lasted several years. Sir Hugh Rose's most important success was the re-capture of Jhansi from the rebels, led by Jantia.

Foley Manor surrounded by its beautiful gardens and the green and pleasant Hampshire countryside, must have been a welcome refuge from the brutal and bloody campaigns in India. As you follow Sir Hugh's gaze across the lilly topped lake, it is hard to imagine a place further removed from the hot, colourful and noisy towns of India where he served.

Stay on the tarmac drive which now leads away from "Foley Manor" with the lake on your right to eventually meet a gate house beside a golf course. Do not continue across the golf course, but take the track left immediately after the gate house. Follow the track which soon ends at the next property, where you should continue ahead now following a narrow path. Ignore all turnings off and stay on the path to arrive at "The Links Hotel" beside the old A3. The hotel which has a crab and lobster restaurant is also a free house offering a wide selection of bar meals and snacks - a perfect place for a rest.

The A3. Being a walker, I like many others resent the intrusion of bigger and faster roads eating into the easily developed countryside. Therefore, it may seem strange that I should choose to talk about a road and a main one at that. The A3 though, has I believe a history worth telling, having over the last three centurie, changed the character of this part of Hampshire.

It was the development of Portsmouth into a major naval base at the end of the 17th century, that saw the rapid growth of the A3. Coaching inns sprung up at regular points along the way, sometimes with communities growing up around them. The original coaches started from the Elephant and Castle in London and would take fourteen hours (if they made it at all), to reach Portsmouth. These would often carry sailors drinking their way from coaching inn to coaching inn, turning many of the tranquil villages into noisy hell holes. Monies being spent on drink, the innkeepers and farmers would often allow the sailors to sleep in their barns or stables at a reduced rate. One can only imagine the smell when a crew after several days of drinking and sleeping in stables, rejoined their ship!

Over the years the road improved and towards the end of the 19th century, a coach could do the journey from London to Portsmouth in under ten hours. At this time, there were no less than twentyfour coaches a day operating the route. One of the best known coaching inns on the road was and still is just up the road in the centre of Liphook, The Anchor. Many important people have stayed here over the years, some of whom were royalty, including Queen Victoria. It was also popular with the less respected, its cellars being used to house wrong-doers who were chained to the walls until their trial. At the end of your walk, you could do a lot worse than to try The Anchor for yourself, though go careful with the local brew as rumour has it that the chains are still in the cellars ready for use!

The A3 has recently been diverted and perhaps thankfully, the road at which you stand is now only a shadow of what it was.

From "The Links Hotel", cross the main road and turn right for a short distance and then left beside a wooden hut, marking the 10th tee of Liphook golf club. Pass to the right of a house, "West View" and follow the track ahead to pass under a railway line, the main line from Portsmouth to London. Thereafter, carry straight on thereby leaving the main track which bears right and follow a grass track ahead ignoring all turnings off.

As a valley opens out on your left, you will soon meet a footpath sign on your right which also marks the boundary between Hampshire and Sussex. You should ignore this and continue straight on where for a short distance you will be walking through Sussex. Shortly after the footpath sign, the path forks. Here you should take the less prominent path left to descend gently into the valley and then follow the valley bottom to later pass through a small plantation of young birch. This eventually leads to a crossing path on to which you should turn left to arrive at a wide track. Turn left to follow the track which is part of the Sussex Border Path. You are now back in Hampshire.

Follow the track ignoring all turnings off for approximately a quarter of a mile to meet a small road (OS. 847304). Cross the road and continue ahead where almost immediately, the path forks and you should take the left and more prominent fork and follow this, again ignoring any turnings off. At a "T" junction turn right and join a wider track, a bridleway, to cross Stanley Common. The bridleway runs straight across the common and later runs above a ditch on your left, probably the original track. The ditch gradually peters out and you should continue straight on along the valley bottom, ignoring turnings off to the left and right, following a prominent track for some distance until you meet a well defined path on your left, signposted as a public bridleway. As a guide, the distance from the "T" junction, our starting point on this track, to the bridleway on the left is approximately one third of a mile.

Turn left to follow the bridleway gently uphill away from the valley bottom. At the top, you will join a wider track where you should continue ahead, i.e. do not turn left, following the sign for the Sussex Border Path once more. On your left at this point as a guide, is a well established chestnut coppice. As you continue you may hear hooting sounds in the distance. This is in fact Hollycombe steam collection, a miniature steam railway, which is only a mile distant.

i

52

The track soon meets a crossing track which you should ignore to continue ahead, still on the Sussex Border Path. You are again, at this point, back in Sussex. Stay on the track ignoring turnings off to the left and right and at a fork take the left hand path, following the public bridleway signs to descend into a valley. At the bottom of the valley you will meet a crossing path on to which you should turn left, again in the direction of the Sussex Border Path sign (**OS. 858307**). This path now runs north along the valley bottom and after a short distance, meets fields on the left and follows their perimeter. Just before a house ahead to your left, a footpath joins from the right. Ignore this to continue straight on still following the Sussex Border Path.

At a junction of paths, leave the Sussex Border Path to take the second path on your left marked as a public footpath. You will now follow a narrow path through bracken to reach the B2131, which you should cross to join the signposted public bridleway the other side. This goes steeply uphill and at the top forks, where you should take the right hand fork, the more defined path, still a public bridleway. As you continue this graduates into a wide track and then a drive way running between large properties. The drive way in turn becomes a tarmac lane.

Follow the lane until you reach the last two properties, "East Lodge" and "Gilhams Farm" and take the public bridleway opposite "Gilhams Farm" and beside "East Lodge". Immediately after joining, bear right through a wooden farm gate and continue along the top of a field to join a narrow path leading to another wooden farm gate through which you should pass. There are good views left at this point across the valley to Cold Ash Hill, so called it is believed, because ash used to be stored here for repairing the roads.

Follow the narrow path, a bridleway, downhill through woodland owned by the Woodland Trust, which in summer is a mass of foxgloves. As you near the bottom of the hill, you should ignore any turnings off and continue straight on. Sometime later, the path becomes more prominent and you will pass a bungalow on your right before meeting two gates ahead of you. Pass through the smaller gate into a field and continue ahead along the left hand perimeter. At the far side of the field cross a stile on to a narrow lane and turn left to head for a small number of houses which form the hamlet of Hammer Bottom.

The lane leads naturally down to a farm house where you should pass through a gate ahead into the farm yard. Cross the farm yard, frequented by a miscellany of ducks and geese and pass through another smaller gate the other side. Thereafter, you should cross a railway line where you should take great care, as this is in the main line from Portsmouth to London.

Foxglove

At the other side, pass to the left of "Hammer Crossing", an old Victorian railway house and continue ahead along a track to pass over a stream. The stream marks the border between Hampshire and Sussex, so you are now once again in Hampshire. Go up the other side of the valley and bear right to pass two houses on your right until you meet a lane opposite "Yew Tree Cottage". To your left here is a welcome break in the form of "The Prince of Wales" pub, which serves Gales Ales and a wide selection of food.

i *Hammer Bottom (OS. 868326 Map 186). Beside The Prince of Wales pub, you are probably at the heart of Hammer Bottom. As the name suggests, this peaceful village was once the centre of the local iron industry. This was started by the Romans who had an encampment nearby. Hammer Bottom was also famous for broom making. These would be made from birch and heather which still grow in profusion in the surrounding hills. The brooms were renowned for their quality and many of them were used in the royal stables.*

To continue our route, turn right along the lane passing the cottages of Hammer Bottom until you pass a white cottage, "Redstock", on your left. Here you should bear left up the drive towards the garage, immediately before which is a signposted public footpath going uphill along the perimeter of the property. In summer this footpath can become overgrown and as a result, there is an alternative route. This is to follow the lane passing "Redstock", until you reach the next property on the left beside a bus shelter. Here you should turn immediately left in front of the bus shelter and follow a track almost back on yourself. As the track bends right you should leave it to continue ahead along a grass track to reach the gate to "Redstock", albeit this time half way along the garden perimeter.

Both routes lead to the garden gate just mentioned, where you should follow the narrow path uphill still along the property perimeter, to shortly reach and pass over a crossing track. Quite soon after, you should ignore another smaller crossing path to continue your climb uphill. On nearing the top you will enjoy your first real views of the walk back over Hammer Bottom. To your left is Haslemere and to your right in the distance Butser Hill. At the right time of year, usually early summer, the hill top is a bloom of purple heathers.

At the top of the hill, ignore a crossing path and carry straight on to sometime after ignore another more prominent crossing path. Eventually, you will meet a very wide track at a clearing and a line of telegraph poles. Turn right here and follow the track lined by the telegraph poles, ignoring a footpath shortly after which joins from the right. The track eventually leads to a car park and a lane. Turn left on to the lane and follow it to meet the busy A3. The lane leads out between a Little Chef restaurant and, at the time of writing, a disued pub, "The Spaniard".

i *Bramshott Camp and Tin Town (OS. 867336 Map 186). Standing beside the busy A3 and the ultra modern Little Chef, it is hard to imagine that you are standing at what was once the centre of a busy army camp. Apart from some old slabs of concrete almost completely covered by grass, there is no sign of the bustling camp which housed the Canadian army during both world wars. The Little Chef was in the First World War the camp H.Q. The currently derelict pub, was known then as The Seven Thorns. Behind this, roughly at the clearing through which we previously passed, was the Canadian general hospital. The other side of the A3, stood a line of ramshackle huts, shops and cafes, mostly built of corregated iron. This quickly became known as Tin Town and even had its own theatre.*

Behind Tin Town were the barracks known as North Camp. The huts which made up the camp each housed twentyfive men. Perhaps understandably, with such a vast gathering of men things were not always easy. The shops at Tin Town were regularly broken into and once, a gang of bank robers were caught underneath a cafe hiding from the military police.

Apart from the sadness of the war itself, one of the sadest moments of Bramshott Camp in World War I, was the outbreak of spanish influenza. At its height, it killed ninety soldiers in one month. The six hundred and thirty bed hospital also treating war casualties, was hard pushed to cope. Thankfully, the outbreak ended as quickly as it began and the camp returned to relative normality.

At the end of the First World War, the army completely cleared the common of all the camp buildings. Bramshott Camp was rebuilt during the Second World War, but not to the same scale. At the end of the Second World War, Huron Camp (situated behind The Spaniard pub) roughly at the site of the hospital of the first war, became a Canadian repatriation centre. Later, it was used by the Womens Royal Army Corps School of Instruction. The camp closed completely in 1966 and everything was demolished.

Ghosts apart, the only easily visible reminders of the Canadians are the sycamores lining the A3 which ran through the centre of the camp. The sycamore leaves reminded the homesick soldiers of their national emblem, the maple leaf. Standing beside the A3 I wonder how many motorists realise the significance of the sycamores, very few I feel and as the years go by, fewer still.

Cross the A3, a dual carriageway taking great care to do so and pass through a gap in the central reservation to join a public bridleway which is signposted the other side. Please note, that the gap in the central reservation is also a turning point for cars so do take care. Follow the bridleway downhill and at the bottom turn right. After approximately thirty paces, the path forks and here you should take the left hand fork in the direction of the footpath sign, to go gently uphill through bracken crossing Bramshott Chase. Pass over a crossing path at the top of the hill and sometime after, ignore a crossing track to continue ahead and arrive at a small gate.

Go through the gate and carry on along a grass path running between two large properties. As you continue, keep to the wall on your left to reach a gravel drive where you should turn left and pass through a small iron gate to follow a signposted footpath. The grass footpath descends gradually running between laurel and rhododendron bushes and eventually meets another metal gate. Pass through the gate and carry straight on, ignoring any turnings off to the left or right, to wind through more dense woodland and bracken. The path later joins a wide track which continues in the same direction downhill.

The track will lead you back to Waggoners Wells where perhaps you can enjoy a final respite to reflect on your day out, before retracing your steps back to the parking area and the commencement of our walk.

ACCOMMODATION

Old Thorns (Kosaido) Hotel, Liphook. Tel: 0428 724555

On the walk, this is a plush hotel owned by the Japanese Kosaido Group. The hotel has a Japanese restaurant and bar, Japanese gardens and even a Japanese bath. If your walk is not enough, the hotel also has an eighteen hole golf course, tennis courts and an indoor swimming pool.

The Links Hotel, Liphook. Tel: 0428 723773

On the walk, this is a relaxed informal hotel which in its heyday entertained many celebrities and even royalty. The hotel which is more of an inn is comfortably furnished with low snug leather chairs in the bar. The rooms are also well furnished.

Youth Hostel, Hindhead YHA, Devils Punchbowl, Hindhead.
Tel: 0428 734285

Three and a half miles from the walk, a simple youth hostel situated in the bowl of the Devils Punchbowl. Basic but idyllic and I loved it. Camping is also permitted.

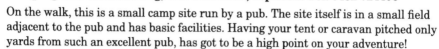
Camping and Caravanning, The Deershut, Liphook. Tel: 0482 724406

On the walk, this is a small camp site run by a pub. The site itself is in a small field adjacent to the pub and has basic facilities. Having your tent or caravan pitched only yards from such an excellent pub, has got to be a high point on your adventure!

THE HIGHLAND FLING

Distance: 13½ miles (21.75 km)
Time: Allow approximately 7½ hours
Map: Ordnance Survey Landranger Map 195

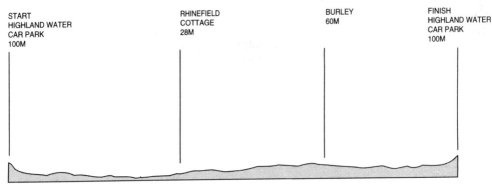

START	RHINEFIELD	BURLEY	FINISH
HIGHLAND WATER	COTTAGE	60M	HIGHLAND WATER
CAR PARK	28M		CAR PARK
100M			100M

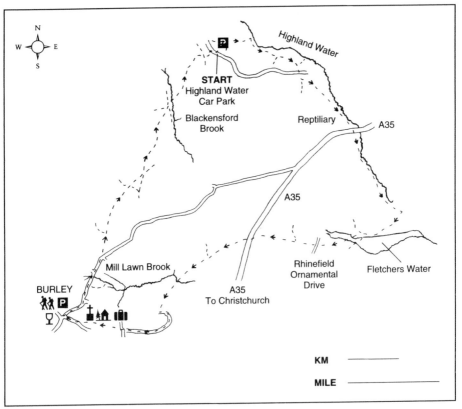

Walk Summary

The Highland Fling takes you through some of the most wooded and remote parts of the New Forest. The scenery is never dull and you will be constantly touched by the charm of this ancient forest. The best time to do the walk is in mid-autumn when the leaves on the trees are a blaze of colour and the deer gather in herds for the rut. Stay alert and tread carefully and you will be rewarded by nature for your efforts.

Two points to remember:-

(1) The paths through the New Forest are, in the main, not public rights of way but managed by the Forestry Commission who in general, try and adopt a freedom to roam policy. There are times however, when certain paths may be closed for the benefit of wildlife. Ensure therefore, you have a map and be prepared to detour from the route.

(2) Paths through the forest can be undefined and difficult to describe. Pay careful attention to the route description and follow the map with care and if you know how to use one, a compass may also be useful. Although I recommend Landranger Map 195, it is a good idea to back this up with the Ordnance Survey Outdoor Leisure Map 22.

Follow these simple rules and you will complete the walk without mishap.

For all the extra effort involved, the beauty of the New Forest is in my opinion, unsurpassed in the south of England and the difficulties which the forest bring are also what make it so enjoyable. Finally, much of the route can be muddy and on occasion, you will need to cross streams which offer neither stepping stones or bridges so come prepared.

Start - OS. 246083 Map 195

The walk starts from the Highland Water car park marked by a blue "P" on the Ordnance Survey map. To get there, if coming from the south west, take the A35 which passes through the centre of the forest. Look out for a turning left signposted to Bolderwood which is Bolderwood Aboretum Ornamental Drive. Follow the drive to its end beside Bolderwood car park and at the "T" junction turn right, signposted to Emery Down. Highland Water car park is the first car park on the left. If coming from the north or west, take the A35 from Lyndhurst heading towards Bournemouth and on reaching The Swan Inn, turn right onto a lane signposted to Emery Down. On reaching Emery Down, continue straight on until you reach The New Forest Inn. Turn left immediately after the inn onto a lane signposted to Bolderwood, Lynwood and Fritham. Follow the lane for approximately two and a half miles to reach Highland Water car park on your right. An alternative start could be the village of Burley (OS. 212031 Map 195).

THE HIGHLAND FLING

Before setting out, please take heed of the New Forest code on the inside back cover of this book.

From the car park go east through a small wooden gate and continue ahead along a narrow but well used path which leads through typical New Forest woodland. This winds downhill and becomes fairly prominent. You should ignore all turnings off to eventually reach a wide track at a "T" junction. Turn right along the track where after a few paces, you will meet a crossing track which you should ignore to continue straight on.

Sometime later, the track forks and our route is along the right hand and less prominent track which shortly bends round to the left. Through the trees on your left as you progress, is a large ditch which is in fact a stream, Highland Water. Stay on the track, later ignoring a crossing track, to eventually meet a junction of tracks, also a large clearing used as a turning point for forest vehicles. The main track turns right here, but you should ignore this to continue straight on along a grass track **(OS. 259082)**. This part of the route is particularly pleasant, being a mass of forest life both vegetation and if you are lucky, animals.

The track soon becomes wider and you should stay on it ignoring all turnings off, for approximately a quarter of a mile until you reach a small wooden gate. Pass through the gate and continue ahead along a now less defined route to meet a lane. A short detour left here, will bring you to The Portugese Fireplace, all that remains of some barracks which housed Portuguese troups during the First World War. To continue our route, cross the lane and at the other side, pass through another wooden gate and continue along a wide track signposted as Holidays Hill Inclosure.

Holidays Hill Inclosure (OS. 264078 Map 195) was inclosed in 1696. Inclosures are required to protect young trees from the deer and ponies. The first inclosures occurred in the 15th century when timber was vital for construction and the shipbuilding industry. The first Act giving the power to inclose parts of the forest was passed in 1482. In 1698, an extension to the Act allowed a further six thousand acres to be inclosed. Another Act in 1949, allowed the current managers, the Forestry Commission, to inclose another five thousand acres for the growing of timber. Up to the present day, approximately half of this figure has been inclosed and planted.

After a short distance the track forks in front of a low fenced pond. Here, you should take the left hand fork which passes through somewhat different woodland predominantly mixed conifers, to eventually arrive at a white cottage. Pass through a gate to enter the grounds in front of the cottage, which is in fact a reptiliary. The round enclosures on your left here contain a number of snakes, lizards and other reptiles which are free to view. On the right, there is information in the form of leaflets or recorded details available on the reptiliary and its inhabitants.

Continue along the drive to exit via a wooden gate and bear left thereafter to pass in front of the cottage, "Holidays Hill Cottage". Follow the drive away from the cottage passing on your way clearings on either side which are the remains of a camp site. At the time of writing, the camp site is out of use but this could change again in the future. Also on the left as you continue, are the steep banks overlooking the picturesque Highland Water.

At the end of the drive pass through a wooden gate to arrive at a main road, the A35. Cross the road and pass through another wooden gate to continue ahead along a somewhat undefined grass track, passing through a mass of deciduous woodland. Ignore all turnings off and follow the main route which winds through the forest in a

A New Forest cottage

southerly direction. Sometime later, you will meet a wooden bridge on the left which crosses Highland Water, a lovely place to stop and rest awhile under the shade of the many trees overlooking the stream. Do not cross the bridge, but continue ahead in the same direction following in the main, Highland Water on your left.

After approximately a quarter of a mile, the stream disappears off to the left for a while and our path continues straight on albeit much narrower, through older and more established forest. It soon rejoins Highland Water, where you should bear right to follow the banks of the stream and shortly after, cross one of its tributaries by way of a wide wooden plank bridge **(OS. 281050).** After the bridge, turn left and follow the tributary to almost immediately rejoin Highland Water and continue along the right hand bank. After a short distance, you will pass a field on the left the other side of Highland Water, which has been given over to conservation and entry is therefore not permitted. If you keep your eyes peeled, this is a good area to spot deer.

i   ***New Forest Deer.*** *It is the deer we must thank for the preservation of the forest. This dates back to Norman times, when William the Conqueror appointed the area as a Royal hunting forest. "Forest" is in fact a Norman expression roughly translated meaning "non productive land".*

Today, there are five species of deer in the forest, Fallow, Muntjack, Red, Roe and Sika, though it is the Fallow deer that you are most likely to encounter. The Fallow deer is easily distinguishable by its white spotted chestnut coat and distinctive white and black rump. If as I recommend, you visit the forest in autumn, you are more likely to hear the deer before you see them. At this time, the rutting season, the male deer the buck, bellows loudly to assert his authority. It can be an alarming sound if you do not expect it. During the rut, the deer gather in herds headed by dominant bucks proudly displaying their fully grown antlers. You may even see a fight between rival bucks. The ferocity of the battle is quite surprising not normally ending until one of the bucks retires injured, although this is seldom serious.

On meeting a wide track, turn right and after approximately ten paces, take the left hand fork thereby leaving the more prominent track. You will now follow a grass path where you should ignore another narrow path off to the right to continue straight on. This soon leaves the wooded area for the first time to cross Poundhill Heath. Follow the grass track which runs across the centre of the heath, passing to the left of a newly planted area which is fenced. After this, continue straight on heading for the tree line ahead.

The track enters the tree line known as Fletchers Thorns and continues ahead through mixed woodland, much of which is initially hawthorne and silver birch. After a short distance, it meets a bridge which crosses Fletchers Water, although on the Ordnance Survey Map it is marked as Black Water. Do not go over the bridge, but turn right immediately before it and walk parallel to Fletchers Water, to shortly pass through a gap in the fence ahead. Continue straight across an open field to pass through a small wooden gate beside a larger one and carry straight on along a wide grass track which runs between fir trees. After a short distance, you will meet a large and prominent gravel crossing track. Here you should continue straight on, bearing slightly left, to join a grass track the other side. Take care not to miss this as the track can at first be slightly undefined.

The track continues straight on through the wood to meet Fletchers Water. There is no bridge across the stream so our route is a mixture of jumping across the pebbled stream bottom and paddling to the other side. Continue straight on at the other side, through beautiful and untouched forest and shortly after, ignore a crossing track to continue ahead. After approximately a third of a mile, you will meet a fork where you should take the left and less prominent track, to reach a road known as Rhinefield Ornamental Drive in front of a cottage, "Rhinefield Cottage" **(OS. 266042).**

Cross the road and continue along a wide gravel track passing to the left of the cottage. Stay on the track, ignoring all turnings off, for a distance of one mile until you once again meet the main road, the A35. Ignore a track off to your left at this point, pass through a small wooden gate and cross the main road. At the other side, turn left for approximately forty paces and then right to pass through a wooden gate into a clearing. Walk up through the clearing to pass through another wooden gate ahead, after which you should carry straight on following a track back into the forest.

After a short distance, the track descends to meet a "T" junction. Here you should turn left to almost immediately meet a crossing track. Pass over the crossing track and continue straight on along a wide track which runs in an almost straight line through conifers. Ignore another crossing track soon after and continue ahead to pass through woodland, now predominantly deciduous. The track soon curves gently right and becomes less prominent. It then bears left again, which you should take care not to miss, to continue in the same original direction with deciduous woodland now on the left and conifers on the right. If you find yourself entering the conifers by way of a small path, then you have gone too far and should retrace your steps. In summer the path can be almost completely overgrown with bracken so take care.

The path though winding, roughly follows the divide between the two types of woodland, until it bears left to run through deciduous woodland to reach a wooden gate beside a fence. The gate marks the boundary of the Old and New Burley Inclosure. Pass through the gate and follow the path the other side which can be very undefined. As a rough guide, you must continue straight ahead until you leave the tree line and meet an open area. Again you should continue straight on, first passing over a small ditch, to follow a narrow path running through heather. There is a somewhat undefined path off to your right at this point which you should ignore. As a guide, if you find yourself following a fence and meeting a gate on the right you have gone too far right. If you have done this, you can rejoin the route by walking directly away from the gate for approximately one hundred metres, until you reach a clearing at a junction of minor paths. Here you should turn right onto a more prominent path, our correct route. You will also have gone too far left if your route follows a ditch.

After a short distance the path widens and meets an open clearing with a number of minor paths off to the left and right. Here you must continue straight on to shortly after the clearing, meet a fork which may not at first be fully visible. Take the left hand path through more heather and bracken and thereafter descend gently through a grove of holly trees and bushes. This will lead you to a clearing with Mill Lawn Brook meandering through its centre in front of you. A lovely spot for a picnic on a summer's day often frequented by many of the New Forest ponies.

The New Forest Ponies. During neolithic times, ponies like the ones in the New Forest roamed freely all over Britain. Over the centuries, they were slowly tamed by man and put to work. Since James I kept a pony for his children, ponies have always been associated with children culminating in the popular Pony Club which now boasts thousands of members.

The New Forest ponies are owned by individuals and roam the land by special arrangement. To classify as a *New Forest pony,* it has to be registered with the *New Forest Pony Breeding and Cattle Society* who ensure that your pony is a perfect breed and not a cross. The *New Forest Verderers,* who are the administrators of the forest, oversee that only true bred stalions and their offspring are allowed to roam free in the forest. To cover the cost of all this, a fee is paid by the pony owner for its right to roam. This is called a *marking fee* and once this is paid, the pony's tail is clipped as a form of licence. The job of marking is a huge one and the majority of it takes place in late summer or autumn, when the ponies are rounded up. This is known locally as *The Drift.* The Drift ties in with the major pony sales of the year including the largest, the *Beaulieu Road Sale.*

New Forest Pony

The ponies appear oblivious to all the officialdom surrounding them and on examining several tails, it looks as though some of them avoid it as well! The main success of the ponies is their ability to eat just about anything. Apart from grass, gorse, holly and ivy, even brambles form part of their diet, enabling them to survive the often harsh winters. Predictably, the most common cause of death is from road accidents and to avoid increasing this you are asked not to feed the ponies no matter how persistent they appear, as this encourages them onto the roads.

From the clearing, you now have a choice of two routes. The first, the shorter route, follows Mill Lawn Brook avoiding Burley to rejoin the main route at Woods Corner (**OS. 220042**). The second, the longer route, takes you into Burley where you can enjoy a drink and perhaps lunch before leaving the village via Woods Corner - the choice is yours.

Short Route via Mill Lawn Brook - To take this route, turn right at the clearing just in front of the bridge and follow the right hand bank of the brook. There is no defined path and your way must be guided by keeping the brook close to your left. After approximately three quarters of a mile, you will meet a wooden footbridge with a handrail allowing passage over the brook. Take this and immediately after, turn diagonally right to meet a lane at a ford. Turn right along the lane and follow it to pass between picturesque cottages, bending round to the left as you continue. Pass "Burley Grange" and keep going uphill until you reach a "T" junction. Turn left for approximately thirty metres and then right on to a gravel track to rejoin the main route (**OS. 220042**).

Long Route via Burley - From the clearing, cross the bridge ahead known as Brooks Bridge and follow the path across heathland heading for the tree line in the distance. It is interesting to note, that the heath you are now traversing is the result of man many centuries ago. Once, this area was all natural forest but as man developed, tree clearing became rife to allow for grazing and crop growing. The poor New Forest soil could only support this practice for a short period of time and when exhausted, man moved on to clear a new area. The result is a vast expanse of heathland.

Ignore all minor paths until you meet the tree line where the path bends left to climb uphill. Here, you should leave the path to continue straight on along a less defined path which shortly runs gently uphill between banks. You will now pass through a grove of holly trees and at the top of the hill, should continue ahead between fences with a field on the right and a large house on the left. The path then joins a drive, the drive to "Markway Lodge" and leads to a lane. Turn left along the lane and continue to shortly pass a clearing on the left complete with post box.

Follow the lane which sweeps round to the right passing a number of lovely cottages and larger properties.

The Burley Dragon. *The lane which is called Bisterne Close, is in a part of Burley once plagued by the Burley Dragon. The story goes that the inhabitants of Bisterne gave the dragon milk to prevent it from eating their sheep. Eventually, the villagers paid a knight to do battle with the dragon. The knight, after fierce fighting, slayed the dragon but not until both his dogs had been killed by the beast. Today, there are several memorials to the dragon including a carving over the entrance to "Bisterne Manor" (private) and a lane officially called Dragons Lane.*

The lane is a long one and it is just over a mile before you arrive at a "T" junction. Turn right here to pass the entrance sign to Burley and thereafter, just after the sign to the "White Buck Inn", turn left along Cott Lane which is in fact a gravel track. Follow Cott Lane passing more properties on the right, one of which is a Youth Hostel, to eventually meet a golf course on the left. The track leads out to the golf club car park where you should bear right to pass in front of the club house and just beyond, the Headquarters of the Burley Scout Group. Continue across a grass area immediately after, bearing left to join a gravel track and carry straight on. The track bends right and then left, where you should leave it to continue ahead crossing the side of a cricket field, heading just to the left of a school building, Burley County Primary School. At the far side of the cricket field, you will meet a road which you should follow ahead to enter Burley proper.

Just before reaching the village centre, look out for an old white milestone on your right, stating "To Lymington. Rest and be thankful" and on another side, "Peace restored 27th March, 1802".

Burley (OS. 212030 Map 195) *today appears a relatively modern village taking full advantage of the many tourists that visit for its obvious charms. Its small bustling centre is aswarm of brightly clothed tourists mingling with inquisitive ponies who hog the bus shelter at the slightest sign of a summer shower.*

The earliest known inhabitants of Burley are from the bronze age who had a settlement on what is now known as Castle Hill. During the Middle Ages the village came under the manor of Richard de Burley. After this, the manor changed hands on numerous occasions. In 1852, the manor passed to Colonel Esdale who pulled down the original house and built the impressive building which stands today, now the Burley Manor Hotel.

The two main industries which have thrived in the village over the centuries until tourism arrived, appear to have been charcoal burning and smuggling. Smuggling in Burley as in the rest of the country, was at its height during the 17th and 18th centuries. Burley being at the centre of a circle of major towns and supported by a labyrinth of forest tracks, was the ideal base for this illicit trade. There are numerous smugglers tales, many of which are associated with the village inn, The Queens Inn (Whitbread). Recently, a secret cellar was discovered under the floor of the Stable Bar, packed with contraband including liquor and pistols, a dangerous combination.

One trade I have not mentioned, is witchcraft but then this is a fairly recent one. During the 1950's, there lived in the village a white witch, a high priestess, *Sybil Leek. Sybil spent much of her life travelling with the true gypsies gaining an intimate knowledge of the forest. This knowledge gave her the ability to mix her herbal potions and to read the seasons and the stars, so essential to her profession. She could often be seen in a sweeping cloak with her jackdaw perched on her shoulder searching the forest for ingredients. So successful was she, she published several books and became a popular television personality. Unfortunately, this was to be her downfall, as the publicity destroyed her private life and to escape it she moved to America. However, her work was not all in vain. The coven of witches which she started, Horsa Coven, still thrives.*

After perhaps a short spell (pun intended!) at "The Queens Head" we can continue our walk by turning right in front of the pub and following a lane, Chapel Lane, leading away from Burley centre. After a short distance, a small road leads off to the right to Burley church, should you wish to visit. Our route however, is ahead along the lane passing a lovely thatched property on the right and thereafter, a number of houses on both sides. Continue past Burley United Reformed Church on the right and carry straight on to cross two small bridges over Mill Lawn Brook, passing a lane off to the left thereafter, signposted to Ringwood.

Shortly after passing "Wayfarers", a white house on the right, the road bends right. Leave the road at this point and take a gravel track still going straight on. If you reach a road off to the right, signposted to Mill Lawn, then you should retrace your steps (approximately thirty metres) to join the gravel track. This is the point at which the alternative shorter route rejoins our walk **(OS. 220042).**

Once on the gravel track, do not make the mistake of turning left but continue straight on to reach a wooden gate. Pass through the gate and follow the track ahead through the now familiar deciduous woodland of the New Forest. After a short distance, you should ignore a wide grass track going off to the left and later a crossing track which is grass off to the right and gravel off to the left. After the crossing track, you must later ignore another grass track which this time joins from the left. After this, the deciduous trees, mainly beech and oak, give way to a small mixture of conifers.

Stay on the gravel track ignoring all other turnings off until you eventually meet a narrow tarmac lane. Cross the lane and join a gravel track the other side, still in the same direction. Ignore the first crossing track and continue for some distance until you meet a second crossing track, more diagonal in appearance, where you should turn left to continue along a grass track. Almost immediately after, you should ignore a turning off to the left to continue ahead going gently uphill. Ignore a crossing track to carry on in the same direction to then pass through the remains of an old boundary, a bank, almost a sign that you are entering the old forest proper.

The track begins to go downhill between banks where either side there are a number of old enclosures. The going here can be extremely wet and muddy and is often strewn with rotting branches and trees. You should continue straight on to reach a grass crossing track. You are now in the heart of deer country and as a consquence, the route ahead is sometimes signposted as a deer conservation area. Therefore, for the sake of the deer access at certain times of the year is forbidden. For this reason, again there is an alternative route. Both routes rejoin at **OS. 238075.**

Main Route - The main route continues straight on over the crossing track (only if there are no "no entry" signs) along a less defined track which soon goes gently downhill. Go over another crossing track where you will now follow a wider grass track to reach a

"T" junction. Turn left here to follow a grass track which soon bends right to cross Blackensford Brook by way of a small wooden bridge. This is a lovely part of the walk and probably one of the last chances to stop and enjoy a rest in peaceful surroundings. After the brook, you will meet a clearing which is in fact an extremely wide fork. Our route is along the right hand fork, i.e. continuing straight on along a grass track intersperced with reeds and therefore often muddy. The scenery here is quite untouched and a good place, if you are lucky, to see deer and also ponies in their natural habitat.

Ignore a crossing track and continue ahead to reach a gravel track, where you should bear right to continue your route straight on. This very quickly meets another gravel track at a "T" junction. Turn left here and after approximately forty paces, turn right on to a grass track which leads downhill to Bratley Water. Here, there is no bridge, so jumping and paddling to cross is the order of the day. Carry straight on up the other side which can be extremely wet and boggy. On reaching the top ignore a track off to the left to join a gravel track ahead, where you should carry on in the same direction, i.e. do not turn right. It is here that the alternative route rejoins our walk (OS. 238075).

Alternative Route - To take the alternative route, at the grass crossing track turn right along the grass track and ignore all turnings off to meet a gravel track at a crossroads. Turn left on to the gravel track and follow it gently downhill, crossing Blackensford Brook soon after. Immediately after the small bridge over the brook, take the first turning right to cross another brook, Bratley Water, by way of a narrow wooden footbridge. At the other side, go straight uphill along a wide grass track, again ignoring all turnings off to reach another wide gravel crossing track. Turn left here and follow the gravel track ahead and ignore any paths off to the left or right. Continue along the track and as it bends sharply right a grass track joins from the left. This is the point at which we rejoin the main route (OS. 238075).

Stay on the gravel track to almost immediately after, ignore a turning off to the right and continue to soon meet a crossing track with a seat. Go over the crossing track and carry straight on along one of the official Forestry Commission circular routes, marked by posts with a coloured stripe. As you progress, you will pass a number of notices detailing information on your surroundings.

The gravel track winds downhill to meet a fork. Take the right hand fork which is uphill, testing your legs for the last time, to meet a "T" junction. Turn right here, still going uphill, to meet a lane which you should cross to continue straight on along a gravel track leading to a white cottage, "Bolderwood Cottage". Opposite the cottage, the track bends left to run between outbuildings and re-enters the forest. It then descends gently and passes between two enormous redwood trees to go through a gate and meet a lane. Turn right along the lane and continue for a short distance until you meet a car park on the left which was our starting point. If you have enjoyed your day out, then I suggest you try and visit the New Forest Museum and Visitors Centre at Lyndhurst. Finally, if you are driving, remember, stay under forty miles per hour on forest roads.

ACCOMMODATION

The White Buck Inn, Burley. Tel: 04253 2264

On the walk, this is a comfortable hotel in a large Victorian house on the outskirts of Burley. The rooms are excellently furnished and in the comfortable lounge a wide range of well prepared meals are served.

The New Forest Inn, Emery Down. Tel: 0703 282329

One and a half miles from the walk, this is one of the best inns in the forest. It is in a beautiful setting and the feel of the forest is not lost in the homely bar. Excellent food.

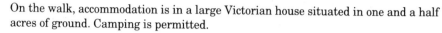 **Youth Hostel, Burley YHA, Burley. Tel: 04253 3233**

On the walk, accommodation is in a large Victorian house situated in one and a half acres of ground. Camping is permitted.

Camping and Carvanning

There are numerous sites throughout the New Forest all run by the Forestry Commission. For a brochure or more information, telephone: 0703 283771.

DROVING FOR GOLD

Distance: 14 miles (22.5 km)

Time: Allow approximately 7 hours

Map: Ordnance Survey Landranger Map 185

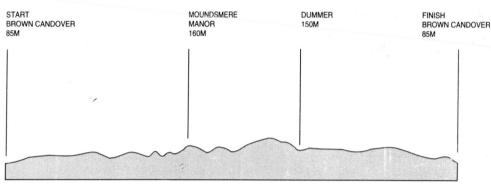

START BROWN CANDOVER 85M	MOUNDSMERE MANOR 160M	DUMMER 150M	FINISH BROWN CANDOVER 85M

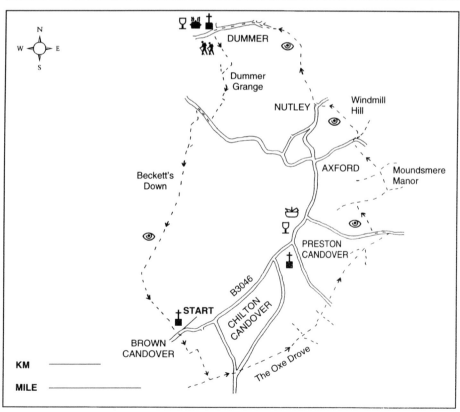

Walk Summary

Droving for Gold takes you through typical Hampshire countryside in the form of the Candover valley. This valley seemingly forgotten by the outside world is known as "The Golden Valley" by locals. This dates back to the wealth the valley once contained, today the "Golden" is more relevant to the corn which covers the valley sides every summer. Even the corn now cannot cover all the farmers expenses however, and the valley has become popular for game shooting. In late summer especially, your route will be busy with pheasants escaping your feet.

Do not expect spectacular scenery or numerous picturesque villages. This is a remote walk through unspoilt countryside where the absence of man allows you to be at one with your surroundings. There are no steep ascents but the walk can seem longer than it appears, so take plenty of refreshments. One final comment, if you can I recommend you make a weekend of it. There is some good accommodation in the valley and staying overnight can only enhance the experience of a truly english community.

Start - OS. 583396 Map 185

The walk starts from Brown Candover opposite St. Peter's church. Parking is simply on the road side and is limited so please be considerate to the local population. To get there, from the south, take the B3046 from New Alresford and stay on the B3046 passing "The Woolpack Inn" to enter Brown Candover itself. Continue until you see St. Peter's church on your left and a mushroom farm on the right. If coming from the north, travel to Basingstoke and follow the signs through the town for the A339 and Alton. After passing under the M3, take the first road right signposted as Farleigh Road and to Cliddesden, Ellisfield, The Candovers and Alresford. This is the B3046. Follow the road for approximately eight and a half miles to reach Brown Candover. An alternative start is from Dummer, though starting here means no lunch time pub stop. The nearest railway station is at Basingstoke.

DROVING FOR GOLD

The walk starts at a track beside "Moth Farm" opposite St. Peter's church. At first it is worth knowing a little about the village from where we begin.

Brown Candover (OS. 583396 Map 185) is one of three Candover villages in the valley. Candover is derived from the celtic word "Dever" which means water crossing. Today, the Candover river has all but dried up, it now only rises just south of Brown Candover feeding the many watercress beds near Alresford, before joining the Alre river. The church of St. Peter is relatively modern. It is a peculiarity of the valley in that its predecessor, like that of its neighbours at Swarraton and Chilton Candover, was pulled down with the only remaining church in the valley at Preston Candover being destroyed by fire. There can be few places in the British Isles where there has been such destruction of the Christian church. The modern St. Peter's is a respectable replacement, of particular interest is the finely carved alter rail, a relic from the original church.

Take the track at "Moth Farm" to enter the farmyard itself where you should continue straight on to shortly pass a tennis court on your right which belongs to "Candover House", just visible beyond. Stay on the track and look out on your right as you progress for an old iron pump in the corner of a field, an unusual relic from the past. Follow the track which soon bends left and later right where it is worth stopping to look back over the church and village of Brown Candover. The track continues until you eventually meet a "T" junction. Turn left here to join an ancient track marked on the map as the Oxe Drove.

The Oxe Drove is one of several ancient tracks that cross Hampshire. They were mostly created by the Celts and became important trading routes as time progressed. Oxe Drove is a generic term for these tracks and gives you an indication of one of the main uses for the routes. This track is also known as the Lun Way which was a famous salt way, transporting salt from the coast to the towns inland. Today, with tinned food and deep freezers it is hard to understand just how important the salt trade was. Then, salt was the only way to preserve meat and was essential if famine was to be prevented. The name Lun Way is probably derived from the Saxon word Lun, which means "popular".

The Oxe Drove is bordered by thick hedges made up of a variety of shrubs and brambles. This is another clue to the age of the track. Hedgerows, especially of the fruit variety, were planted as a source of food for landowners and travellers alike. If you are walking this way in late summer or autumn, you definitely will not go hungry. Sloe, elderberries and blackberries are in abundance.

Follow the track gently uphill where it becomes more prominent, passing a small wooden property on the right. Carry straight on, ignoring all turnings off, to eventually meet a lane. Cross the lane and continue ahead to join the track opposite signposted as a right of way. After approximately twenty metres, you will meet another lane which again you should cross to continue ahead still on a right of way. The track is now grass and still part of the Oxe Drove.

The track goes downhill and then begins a long gentle climb uphill still lined by trees and hedges. It later suddenly opens out in front of a large attractive house with its drive sweeping off to the left. This is just one of the many manor houses which dot the valley the remains of the golden age. Across the other side of the valley another manor house is visible, "Chilton Manor". Go straight on along the tarmac drive where the track to your right leads past an old mill stone to Juniper Hill. Pass in front of the house where immediately after, you will pass an ornate conservatory complete with an attractive tower topped by a weather vein.

The sudden break in the scenery ends just as quickly as you leave the property behind to continue on the hedgerow bordered Oxe Drove. A grass track leading off to the left later gives a small break in the undergrowth. Do not turn left but continue ahead to later pass a signposted footpath on your right which leads to Upper Wield, a fairly long detour if you decide to visit the village. Our route however, remains along the Oxe Drove where a few paces on, another footpath leads off to the left, this too you ignore.

Soon after the footpaths, the Oxe Drove meets a crossing track in front of a small beech copse. You should ignore the crossing track and continue straight on for approximately half a mile to meet a lane. Here there are more scenic views of the surrounding countryside and to your right a large barn. If you are particularly thirsty then you can turn left along the lane for one mile, to visit Preston Candover where you will find "The Purefoy Arms", a Courage pub. The village also has a General Stores. Our route however, takes us across the lane to continue ahead along the Oxe Drove still signposted as a right of way. You should ignore all turnings off. As you continue, the track becomes far more open with views to your left over the rooftops of Preston Candover and "Preston Grange Farm".

The track then dips before going uphill again and crosses the centre of a field which is in fact the top of Preston Down. Carry straight on heading for a group of beech trees ahead, ignoring a footpath off to the left and just after, another off to the right. You are still following the Oxe Drove.

Shortly after the beech trees, the track bends round to the left. Though not a designated footpath, it is easier to follow this to reach a lane where you should turn right for approximately forty metres, until you meet a farm gate with a smaller gate beside it on your left (OS. 624419). Here you should turn left through the small gate to continue our route. If you prefer to keep to designated footpaths and our official route, then leave the track as it bends left to continue straight on along a smaller track passing through a line of trees to meet the lane in front of a cottage. Turn left along the lane for approximately a quarter of a mile, until you meet the small wooden gate mentioned earlier, this time on the right (OS. 624419). Pass through the wooden gate and go straight uphill along a hedged track between fields where at the top the track meets a cross roads. This is a good place to stop to catch your breath awhile and enjoy the views.

Ignore the crossing track and continue straight on to soon go downhill. At the bottom of the valley you should turn right to follow a narrow footpath between hedgerows. If, in summer, this is overgrown then simply follow the right hand perimeter of a field running parallel to the footpath on the left and rejoin the footpath later at an appropriate opening in the hedgerow. Follow the footpath for approximately half a mile which, as you continue, runs between banks until you meet a prominent track left going uphill. Take this track to climb gently uphill between hedges and fields beyond. As you near the top, the hedges give way to open fields on your left and iron fencing on your right. Here you have views right to the manor house, "Moundsmere", one of the larger manor houses of the Candover valley.

The track leads out on to the drive way to "Moundsmere" beside the gates on your right. Go straight across the drive and join a farm track ahead, signposted as a bridleway, passing a small pond on your right. The concrete track soon bends round to the right. You should ignore this and carry straight on to pass through a small wooden gate into a small field or paddock. Go across the field keeping to the left hand perimeter and pass through another small wooden gate the other side to join a bridleway going downhill between hedgerows. This can be somewhat overgrown in summer and protective clothing against nettles is advisable.

The bridleway leads down to a lane on to which you should turn right for approximately twenty metres and then left on to a signposted public bridleway. This passes to the left of a beautiful thatched cottage before bending left to go uphill between fields. The large wood on your right at this point is Nortons Wood, owned by the Forestry Commission. The track bends left again to follow the right hand perimeter of a field becoming steeper as you climb to the top of Windmill Hill. As you progress, you will be rewarded with ever widening views over Hampshire.

The track soon enters another field, still following the right hand perimeter and continues to enter a third field where it begins to descend. To your right here, as a guide, a water tower is visible in the distance. As you descend you will see a small number of houses which make up the hamlet of Nutley, our next destination. Continue downhill to meet a road, the B3046, on to which you should turn left through the centre of the hamlet. After a short distance, look out for a track on your right signposted as a bridleway to Dummer and as a footpath to Oakley and Inkpen Beacon. Cross the road and take this which intially runs beside an old and no longer used cemetery, the other side of a flint wall.

Go through a white metal gate and take care not to make the mistake of going straight on. Bear right immediately after the gate to pass to the right of some farm buildings and follow the track as it climbs gently uphill between the flanks of Nutley Wood. Sometime later, you should ignore a large crossing track to continue ahead along a now grass track.

Soon after, the track enters woodland to become a narrow path climbing uphill through Nutley Wood. After a short distance, the path turns left to run between a line of trees with fields either side and eventually meets a grass track beside a metal gate on the left. This point is known as Dummers Clump (**OS. 603460**), where yet again there are more good views. Carry straight on along a prominent hedged track going gently downhill, to soon pass between cottages, part of "Clump Farm", before meeting a lane.

Do not turn right but go straight on along the lane and follow it for approximately three quarters of a mile to enter the village of Dummer.

Dummer (OS. 588460 Map 185) can after your long trek along the Oxe Drove be a refreshing sight and not just because of its popular pub! The village is made up of two streets, Up Street and Down Street. These are bordered by picturesque cottages from several periods, their past trades now remembered in house names. The village hostelry may well be your first port of call. This is "The Queens Inn", a Courage pub, which apart from food also offers its own cocktail, "The Fergie Fizz", referring to Sarah Ferguson who was once married to Prince Andrew. The Ferguson family home is just outside the village at "Dummer Down Farm". Near the pub is the old village well with its well preserved tread-wheel.

Close to the church is "Dummer House", once the home of the Terry family who were great friends of the Austen family, of literary fame. The church itself which we pass on entering the village, has a number of interesting features. You cannot miss the first as you enter, where a large wooden gallery rises above your head. In the days before organs, this is where a small orchestra would have been seated. The second, is a magnificent rood or cross canopy, in a state of near complete preservation and the only one in Hampshire. Its existence is even more unique, for all such canopies were ordered to be destroyed in the 16th century. Perhaps the greatest treasure though, is the pulpit. This dates from 1380 and is one of the oldest in England. Try and imagine the sermons and advices delivered to the parishoners over the centuries from this pulpit. Many would have been political as well as religious.

One man who regularly spoke from the pulpit stands out from all others. His name was George Whitefield, a follower and companion of the most famouse preacher, John Wesley. The villagers must have thought well of him for Whitefield in a letter to Wesley, after to returning to his home in Oxford, records that he had just left "a weeping flock at Dummer".

By the many memorials in the church you cannot help but notice another family name, that of the Dummer family. The Dummers were lords of the manor from Norman times until the 16th century when the last of the Dummers, William, was laid to rest in the church.

Our route leaves the village along a track just after the church and opposite a small bus shelter. The track is signposted to "Manor Farm" and as a right of way. It is also part of the Wayfarers Walk. Follow the track straight through the farm where after the farm buildings, it becomes concrete and leads downhill between open fields. At the bottom of a shallow valley ignore a track off to the right and continue straight on up the other side. At the top, ignore another track off to the left and continue on still on the concrete track, which shortly bends right. Here the track is no longer concrete but more of a traditional farm track. You should ignore another track which goes straight on and follow the farm track, signposted with the black arrows of the Wayfarers Walk, as it runs along a small ridge with views over the valley on your left. It later bends left where you should ignore yet another track going off to the right.

Continue down to a small group of houses, estate houses to "Dummer Grange", and take a track right in front of the houses, signposted as a right of way. After a short distance, the track bends left where there are views left of "Dummer Grange" itself. Shortly after, you will meet the drive way to "Dummer Grange" on to which you should turn right to head for "Dummer Grange Farm", visible ahead. Follow this to eventually pass over a cattle grid between houses to arrive at a lane.

Turn right along the lane, thereby leaving the Wayfarers Walk, and follow this for approximately three hundred metres, until you meet a large metal farm gate on the left. Go through the gate and continue straight on to meet a track at the edge of a field. Turn left along the track and follow the left hand perimeter of the field round until it eventually leaves the field to enter woodland, Lower Down Copse. Here you should ignore a track off to the right and carry straight on. Beware, the track can be particularly slippery and muddy in wet weather. Ignore all turnings off and follow the track which in summer is lined with brambles and if you are lucky, wild strawberries. It is also a haven for butterflies.

After passing some beehives, slightly hidden, on your right you will arrive at a "T" junction. Turn right along a more prominent track which is again part of the Wayfarers Walk and continue to soon reach an open field. Here you should turn left on to a grass track, still in the direction of the black arrows of the Wayfarers Walk. Take care not to miss it. This track is tree lined and runs gently uphill between fields. After some distance, the track comes out onto open hillside, Becketts Down. From here there are excellent views south across a Hampshire of rolling fields and scattered woodland. Continuing, you should ignore all turnings off, to shortly pass a small chalk quarry on your right. The track now makes a gradual descent along the left hand perimeter of a field.

Raspberry

Maintain your route straight on alongside more open fields to sometime later pass a line of beech trees on the left, after which the track becomes hedged. Continuing downhill you will eventually meet a more prominent track, which you should follow heading for a house ahead, "Lone Barn". Turn left at "Lone Barn" passing through the gate to the property on to the gravel drive and pass to the left of the house, continuing straight on. At the far side of the garden, pass through a wooden gate and continue ahead along a tree lined path, known as Church Lane. This eventually leads you to a wide concrete track leading to some farm buildings on your left which are part of Brown Candover Estate. Go straight over the track and continue ahead along a tree lined path. As you continue, breaks in the hedgerow allow you views to the right of Totford church and left over the northern stretch of the Candover valley.

The path later begins to descend gently to eventually reach a stile beside St. Peter's at Brown Candover. Go over the stile and follow a fenced path beside the church yard to meet a cricket and playing field. Follow the right hand perimeter of the cricket field to meet the B3046 from where we started our walk.

ACCOMMODATION

The Woolpack Inn, Totford. Tel: 0962 732101

One and a quarter miles from the walk, this is an old drovers inn where the cattle or sheep would have been fed and watered in nearby fields, whilst the drovers would make merry and sleep at the inn. In the hunting season, the pub takes on a cosmopolitan feel with visitors from all over the world testing the inn's hospitality before the next shoot. Apart from comfortable accommodation, the inn serves up good beer and satisfying meals. It is also on the Wayfarers Walk and popular with hikers doing the route, so be prepared to be humbled!

Purefoy Arms, Preston Candover. Tel: 0256 389258

One mile from the walk, this is a popular local pub offering accommodation in another of the Candover villages.

Several House, Swarraton. Tel: 0962 734582

Two and a half miles from the walk, a warm welcome is extended at a large Edwardian country house set in twenty acres of well kept grounds. The rooms are huge and the whole house is exceptionally well decorated. In the grounds you can enjoy croquet as well as tennis and for the less sporting, "The Woolpack Inn" is just down the road!

Youth Hostel, Overton YHA, Overton. Tel: 0256 770516

Six miles from the walk, this is a basic but pleasant hostel in what was once the local village school. Set in the heart of the village, there are a number of good pubs within walking distance for your evening's entertainment. Camping is also permitted.

THE ROUNDHEAD ROUND

Distance: 14½ miles (23 km)

Time: Allow approximately 8 hours, more if you wish to fully explore the villages.

Map: Ordnance Survey Landranger Map 185

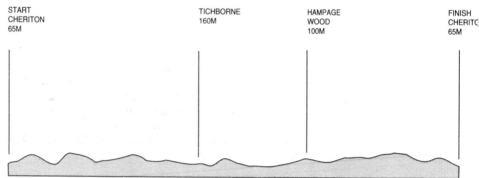

START	TICHBORNE	HAMPAGE	FINISH
CHERITON	160M	WOOD	CHERITO
65M		100M	65M

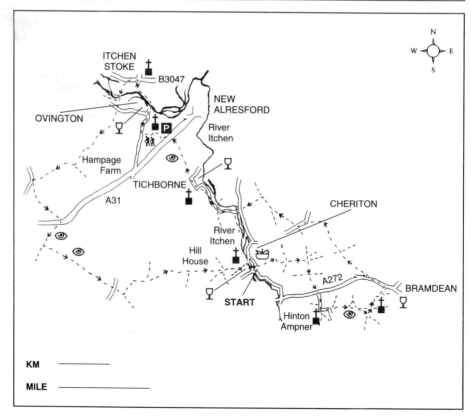

Walk Summary

You should really ensure that you make this walk a full day out. The countryside through which you pass is some of the best Hampshire has to offer, with the villages more than equal to it. Apart from the beauty, the wealth of history that encompasses the walk will more than satisfy the most demanding explorer's interest. Approximately one third of the walk follows the beautiful Itchen valley and its many painted villages, with the other two thirds exploring the Hampshire Downs, wild in comparison to the valley. There are no steep ascents, but some of the paths can be very muddy and the final stages over Gander Down can be energy sapping.

Start - OS. 583285 Map 185

The walk starts from Cheriton village which is on the B3046 between New Alresford and the A272. If coming from the A272, the turning to Cheriton which is signposted, is opposite a garage just south of "Hinton Ampner House", NT. From the other direction, you actually have to go into New Alresford town centre to reach the B3046 and follow it over the A31 to Cheriton. Parking around the village green is limited so please park with consideration. An alternative starting point is from a layby on the north bound carriageway of the A31 (OS. 564312). The nearest railway station is at Winchester, the railway at New Alresford is a steam line (The Watercress Line) and is not connected to the main BR network.

THE ROUNDHEAD ROUND

Starting from the centre of the village, it is worth finding out a bit about our immediate surroundings.

Cheriton (OS. 583285 Map 185) is an idyllic place to start our walk. The village is typical of many on the river Itchen, pretty thatched cottages mingle with grander houses around a village green through the middle of which runs the river itself, at this point only slightly bigger than a stream. The last time I visited, a Kingfisher was sitting on the bank amongst the ducks waiting patiently for its breakfast. The tranquility of the scene is in contrast to one in the 17th century when Cheriton was at the centre of one of the bloodiest battles in the Civil War. Our route later passes through the battle field. The site of Cheriton has seen human habitation since celtic times though the first true records of the village do not begin until 1167. The church dates from about the same period and still has its original tower.

Truffle hunting, normally associated only with France, was once common at Cheriton, indeed it is claimed that Cheriton was the last place in England where truffle hunting was practiced as an industry. Truffles are not on the menu but "The Flower Pots Inn", a free house, serves up some well cooked food as well as real ale. For a packed lunch, there is the Post Office which doubles as a General Store.

To start the walk make your way to the Post Office, which is opposite Cheriton Garage on the eastern side of the green. Make sure you have not had too big a breakfast as a sign on the small road bridge warns that it cannot carry weight beyond normal traffic! From the Post Office follow the lane passing the Post Office on your left and walking away from the village green. The lane soon bends round to the left where you should turn right over a small brick bridge to cross another arm of the river Itchen. Immediately after, turn right to pass Cheriton Primary School and follow the lane to its end. Turn left here along a narrow fenced path, signposted as the Itchen Way and also the Wayfarers Walk and follow it uphill as it runs between properties and gardens. After the houses, the path continues uphill between fields which in summer are a mass of wild flowers.

At the top of the hill, the path opens out into a field where you should continue ahead keeping to the right hand perimeter. Here you will enjoy excellent views of the surrounding countryside. At the far side of the field, cross a stile into another field and turn right to follow the field perimeter round to meet a stile in the far right hand corner (you may wish to take a short cut, going diagonally right across the field). Go over the stile and continue straight ahead along a track in the direction of the black arrows of the Wayfarers Walk and ignore all turnings off to the left and right.

i   **The Battle of Cheriton 1644.** *The track you are on is known as Upper Lamborough Lane and marks the spot of some of the bloodiest fighting seen during the Battle of Cheriton. The battle was one of the most important in the Civil War, some say it was the decisive battle and marked the eventual defeat of the Royalists. The Royalist army led by Lord Hopton, based themselves in nearby Alresford. The Roundheads led by Sir William Waller, hid in Cheriton Wood ahead of you and south around Hinton Ampner. Sir William himself stayed with Lady Stewkeley at "Hinton Ampner House".*

At the beginning of the battle the Royalists had advanced and taken up positions along Upper Lamborough Lane and around Cheriton Wood. The first real fighting took place in the wood itself and resulted in an early victory for the Royalists. Spurred on by this, the cavalry, against orders, charged against the main Roundhead forces massed in the valley below where the A272 now runs. Waller however, who had a reputation for quick thinking, had predicted this and the cavalry ran into an ambush. Virtual slaughter followed and Hopton seeing their fate, followed up with the bulk of his army to try and rescue the situation. With each army having approximately ten thousand men, the battle was fierce and spread far and wide as groups from each side tried to escape or out flank the other. One such group, the Hambledon Boys (see the Mean Meon Meander), played an important role launching a surprise attack on the Royalist's rear flank.

Eventually, the Roundheads gained the upper hand and the Royalists retreated back up to Lamborough and Upper Lamborough Lane where you are now standing. It was here that the retreating Royalist army was attacked from behind. Panic set in as desperate men fought in vain for their lives, the carnage was such that locals claimed the Lamborough lanes ran red with blood that day. The remains of Hopton's army eventually retreated to Alresford which they looted and burned before retreating to Old Basing and then Reading. Skirmishes between die hard Royalists and Roundheads continued for several days before the dead could be buried. Of these there were two thousand men, the majority of them were placed in mass graves below the ground on which you are standing and in the surrounding fields. Nearby are several mounds, evidence of the burials.

The battle effectively ended the Royalist domination of Hampshire, though the garrisons at Winchester castle and Basing both held out for over a year after, sending out sorties and in some cases even defeating the Roundheads. In the end, Cromwell himself led his new Model army to take Winchester and Basing. These are separate stories and worth pursuing another day. Today the screams of battle are replaced by the more pleasant sound of birds singing in the hedgerows, a sound all of the fighters would have known well.

Perhaps now a littled chilled, continue along Upper Lamborough Lane to meet a crossing track where you should turn right in the direction of the black arrow. The track goes uphill for a short distance and then starts to descend quite rapidly. Ahead of you now at the other side of the valley, are the gardens of "Hinton Ampner House", owned by the National Trust.

Stay on the track still going downhill and ignore a crossing track sometime later to continue ahead. The track becomes more prominent as you go and passes a brick cottage on the left to eventually meet the main road, the A272. Cross the road and continue uphill along the lane directly opposite. If however, you wish to visit "Hinton Ampner House", you should turn right along the A272 and then first left.

Hinton Ampner House (OS. 597275 Map 185), as previously mentioned, now belongs to the National Trust. There has been a manor at Hinton Ampner since Norman times, though the first recorded house was built around 1550, on the said site of the original manor which was burned down during the dissolution of the monasteries. The house was in the hands of the Stewkeley family at the time of the Battle of Cheriton. By this time only Lady Stewkeley and her children lived in the house, her husband having died in 1642. Lady Stewkeley favoured the Royalists and not only had to suffer being host to the Roundheads General, Sir William Waller, but watched the Royalists' bloody defeat from the windows of the house. Parliament later seized the house in 1649 and Lady Stewkeley left to marry General Ogle, later to be Viscount Ogle who commanded the castle at Winchester from where the Royalists prepared for the Battle of Cheriton. Hinton must have held sad memories for Lady Stewkeley, for even after King Charles came to the thrown she declined to return to the house. The house was eventually purchased by one Edward Stawell, nephew to Sir Edward Stawell who was one of the cavaliers captured at the Battle of Cheriton. Perhaps the purchase was sweet revenge.

In 1793 the house sadly had to be demolished after its tenants had been forced out by ghosts. Several attempts were made by the Stawell family to re-inhabit the house, but the hauntings were too strong. On demolition a box was found under the floorboards containing a small skull. Locals at the time believed this was the head of a bastard child killed by its parents, Lord Stawell and Honoria Stewkeley. It is believed the ghosts were those of the parents venting their remorse. Happily the hauntings have now stopped.

Two more houses were built and destroyed over the centuries, the current house is very recent, built in 1960. It is now the gardens which people come to visit. The rear lawn and

Original church entrance Ovington

terrace overlook a valley from which the official source of the river Itchen rises. Do not however, form romantic pictures of crystal waters springing from a rock, the source is recognisable only from some very marshy ground which you and I would call a bog.

Returning to our route, follow the lane uphill into the village of Hinton Ampner. The lane runs alongside "Hinton Ampner House" and soon bends left beside a smaller lane. The latter, should you wish to take a small detour, leads to Hinton Ampner church and is also the course of the Wayfarers Walk. The church which is basically Saxon, is worth a detour if only to see the magnificent memorials to some of the inhabitants of Hinton Ampner, including the Stewkeleys. Our route however, follows the lane round thereby leaving the Wayfarers Walk. Stay on the lane until it bends right beside the entrance on your left to "Manor Farm". Turn left here leaving the lane, and follow the drive to "Manor Farm", which is also signposted as a bridleway.

As the drive way bends right, you should leave it to continue straight on following a track ahead and ignore another track which goes off to the left soon after. The track now runs along the right hand perimeter of a field where there are good views across the valley to your left. Continue to the end of the field and pass through a gap in the hedge to follow the track into a second field. At the far side, the track twists right to follow the left hand perimeter of a third field, where there are good views to the south or your right.

At the end of the field just before a copse ahead and on coming level with the tree line on your right, look out for a left turn across the centre of another field which is marked as a footpath. Take this across the centre of the field and on reaching the far side, do not turn right but carry straight on along the right hand perimeter. This leads gently downhill where at a corner of the field you will meet a kissing gate. Pass through the gate and follow the right perimeter of the next field, ahead in the distance to your left is "Bramdean Manor". Pass through another kissing gate soon after and continue ahead along the left hand perimeter of a field heading for a church yard in front of you.

Pass through a kissing gate and carry straight on following the left hand perimeter of the church yard to soon meet a stone path constructed from old headstones. Follow this to reach the front of the church, dedicated to the Saints Simon and Jude.

Bramdean Church (OS. 609278 Map 185) is after such a beautiful approach no disappointment. The church dates from Norman times when the village was still known by its Saxon name, Bradandene, meaning "broad valley". The quaint wooden bell tower is medieval as are the chancel and nave. One of the most attractive parts of the church is its ancient rafter roof. The church is close to the Pilgrims Way which ran from Winchester to Canterbury and was probably a regular stop for the pilgrims. In more turbulant times, the church was near the centre of the Battle of Cheriton, indeed a separate battle took place in Bramdean, known as the Bramdean Fight. The manor house, adjacent to the church, was built in 1740. Centuries before this, the previous house belonged to the disgraced priory at Selbourne (see The High Hanger Hike).

Leave the church yard and continue ahead along a lane going downhill. Shortly after, you will pass a footpath off to the right. This is not part of our route, but leads down to "The Fox Inn", Marstons and is a worthy detour. The inn is over four hundred years old and has a sign depicting its pride in having given shelter and hospitality to the Prince of Wales, later to become King George IV in 1780. The inn may be an early but welcome stop to partake in some of the hospitality for which it is famed.

Typical Hampshire Headstone

The lane eventually leads down to the main road, the A272, where you should turn left to follow the road with care for approximately a quarter of a mile. On reaching a bus stop and on coming level with "Highway Cottage" opposite, cross the road to take a track between "Highway Cottage" on the left and a brick cottage on the right. Follow the track which bends gently left and ignore another track soon after which leads off to the right. Continue straight on behind the houses of Bramdean and thereafter, cross country between fields.

78

The track leads steadily uphill where as you progress, gaps in the hedgerow allow excellent views left across the valley. At the crest of the hill the track enters Cheriton Wood and you should ignore a footpath off to the left. It then immediately begins to descend through the wood where Sir William Waller hid his troops. The views to your left now are over the Itchen valley. The track leaves the wood at the bottom of the valley and soon after, passes a small pond on the left. You should stay on the track and continue uphill between fields until you reach two farm gates beside each other on the left (OS. 598295). If you find yourself passing beneath some electricity pilons, then you have gone too far and should retrace your steps to find the farm gates.

Pass through the second farm gate and follow a track along the left hand perimeter of a field. At the far side of the field pass through a gate onto a lane where you should continue straight on. After a short distance, you will meet a crossing track with a barn on the left. Turn right here to follow the track between fields later passing under the electricity pilons mentioned earlier. After this, the track descends gently to meet another track coming in from the left. If you are observant you may have noticed that there are many tracks in a comparitively small area of land. This is because during medieval times the whole area was one big common and the tracks were lanes providing access for grazing. Some of the hedgerows bordering the tracks also date from this time. The area for centuries attracted many travellers and just two miles west of here at Bramdean Common, the local inhabitants built a small church known as The Gypsy Church for use by the travellers.

Ignore the track joining and continue ahead now going uphill. At the top of the hill you will meet another track off to the left which this time you should take ignoring the black arrow pointing ahead. Follow the track downhill between fields heading for some houses in the distance, one of which is "Cheriton Mill". At the bottom of the hill you will meet a road, the B3046, which you should cross to join a lane opposite. Follow the lane ahead to cross the river Itchen by way of a succession of three bridges and pass "Cheriton Mill" on the left. After the mill, ignore a footpath going off to the left (the Wayfarers Walk and also the Itchen Way) and stay on the lane which later bends right in front of some farm buildings and in particular, a lovely old timber and flint house. Again, you should ignore a signposted footpath left which leads through a farm yard.

Continue along the lane until you pass the sign for Tichborne village. Just after this, take a narrow and somewhat hidden footpath on your left which climbs up a bank between trees. This leads you to a stile which you should cross into a field. Go straight across the field heading, as a guide, to the right of some farm buildings or directly for two white cottages ahead. At the far side, leave the field via a stile and turn left along a lane to follow it as it bends right in front of "Grange Farm" with its magnificent 17th century farmhouse. Welcome to Tichborne.

Tichborne (OS. 571302 Map 185) is yet another idyllic Itchen village. The main street is bordered by unspoilt thatched cottages, north east across the river Itchen itself stands the manor and to the south west the village church stands proud on a hill. A narrow path leads right from the main street to a chapel to the manor. The manor house itself (which is private) is a magnificent affair. It was built in 1803 on the site of the previous house, indeed a manor house has stood on this site since at least the 13th century. The house has always been the seat of the Tichborne family who have lived in the area from the 12th century. Even in Tudor times, the house had a private chapel and it is believed that Henry VIII held one of his marriages here. The house has a beautiful tuscan column porch from where the Tichborne dole is distributed to the villagers every Lady Day.

The Tichborne dole dates back to the 13th century, thereby being the oldest recorded dole handout in the country. Its origin is due to the kindness of Lady Mabella Tichborne who lived in the house in the 13th century. On her death bed she asked her husband, Sir Roger, if he would in rememberance of her, donate to the villagers a dole of bread or a gallon of flour on Lady Day (25th March) for as long as the village of Tichborne remained. Sir Roger, obviously nervous of the expense and believing his wife to be too weak to move, agreed to donate all the corn in the fields his wife could get round whilst a brand (torch) was burning. The gallant lady succeeded in crawling around a twentythree acre field just north of the house. Sir Roger kept his word and to this day the Tichborne dole is handed out every Lady Day. The field providing the corn for the dole is now appropriately known as The Crawls. Only once did the dole stop, when during the late 18th century, imposters from other villages virtually caused a riot to get their free bread.

To maintain the charity, Lady Mabella put a curse on anybody who discontinued the dole. The curse warned that the Tichborne who stopped it would find that his house would fall down and would be born a generation of seven daughters. Shortly after the dole stopped in the 18th century, part of the house did fall down and the successor to the title, Sir Henry Tichborne, produced seven daughters. Needless to say, the dole was quickly reinstated. From this unfortunate event stems another story, that of the Tichborne Claimant. In the late 19th century, the heir to the Tichborne seat should have been Roger Tichborne, the nephew of Sir Henry. Unfortunately, he was lost at sea (did the curse extend this far?) leaving no obvious heir. However, a young man suddenly made a claim to the title, stating that he was Roger Tichborne and had not as others believed, drowned. A trial ensued and eventually the claimant was found to be an imposter, Arthur Orton, the son of a Wapping butcher. He was sentenced to fourteen years imprisonment and forced labour, which included the building of Portsmouth docks.

The Tichbornes were once victim to another curse. It is said that in the 17th century a gypsy woman on being refused charity at the house, put a curse on the child, Richard Tichborne, warning that on a certain day he would drown and be lost. On this day, fearful of the curse, the family had the servants take the boy up on the downs well away from the river. Unfortunately, unnoticed he slipped from the cart and drowned in a water logged track.

If curses were not enough, the Tichbornes always an important family, were deeply involved in the politics of the country often with tragic results. In 1586, Chidiock Tichborne, was found guilty of plotting with Thomas Babington to murder Elizabeth I and put Mary Queen of Scotts on the throne. Consequently, he was sentenced to a slow and painful death. In 1644, the Tichbornes took the side of the King against Cromwell. Again, they backed the wrong side and the Baronet, Sir Benjamin Tichborne had to hide in a hollow tree to escape from the victorious Roundheads.

Appropriately, the striking 11th century church on the other side of the Itchen, has many magnificent memorials to the Tichborne family. The most prominent memorial is a colourful alabaster monument to Sir Benjamin Tichborne and his wife. This is in the north aisle separated by some splendid iron railings from the rest of the church. This unusual arrangement also acts as a catholic chapel and makes St. Andrews church one of only two in England wtih facilities for worship to both the Anglican and Roman Catholic faiths, a measure of the importance and favour of the Tichborne family. Amongst the many other grand memorials is one to the unfortunate child, Richard, who drowned in a rut on Gander Down. Touched by so much turbulant history and the Tichborne monuments, this beautiful church has a presence matched by few others.

In the heart of the village is "The Tichborne Arms", a free house with the Tichborne coat of arms as its sign. It is an appropriate place to enjoy a refreshing drink and a bite to eat.

To continue our route, carry straight on through the village passing the path on the right to the chapel and then another lane off to the left which leads to St. Andrews church. As the lane you are on bends right, you should leave it to take a track off to the left. Follow the track, ignoring a footpath off to the left leading back to the church and follow the side of a house and garden and thereafter continue between fields. Soon after, you will pass a footpath off to the right which leads back to Tichborne.

The track goes steadily uphill where you should ignore a track off to the left to reach the top and enjoy good views back over the Itchen valley and Tichborne. At the end of the field, follow the track as it twists right and then left to continue straight on along the left hand perimeter of the next field, with views to your right now of New Alresford, famous for its watercress. At the end of the field, pass through a wooden gate to reach the busy A31, a dual carriageway. Cross the road with care and join a lane the other side, which immediately bends round to the left. This was part of the original A31 but is now used as a parking area.

Follow the lane until you meet a signposted public footpath on the right which you should take. This is also signposted as the Itchen Way and winds through woodland to soon lead out on to a track. Here you should carry straight on going gently downhill, to meet a field where you should continue along the right hand perimeter. Follow the perimeter to later pass a beautiful cottage on the right and continue ahead along a path to leave the field by descending a bank to meet a lane.

Turn right along the lane, still following the yellow arrow of the Itchen Way and continue following a flint wall on your right which conceals "Ovington Manor". The lane leads you into Ovington village.

The Bush Inn

Ovington (OS. 561317 Map 185) runs gently down a narrow lane to the river Itchen, now truly a river. Like other Itchen villages, Ovington too is made up of unspoilt cottages. The village church was built in 1866 on the site of a previously Norman church, a small arch which was the original entrance to the Norman church still stands in the church yard. A field on the outskirts of the village is known as Butchers Close. It is believed that this is where animals were slaughtered to feed the Royalist army during the Battle of Cheriton.

At the bottom end of the village on the banks of the river Itchen, stands one of the best inns in the country, "The Bush Inn", a free house. The name "The Bush" relates back to times when there were no licencing laws. In those days the hanging of a bunch of twigs or a bush outside a house, indicated the home owner was selling ale. The inn is in a delightful setting and its interior is equal to its surroundings. A stop here is a must!

Follow the lane through the village ignoring a lane off to the left to continue your route downhill. At the bottom of the hill cross over a small stream by way of a brick bridge, after which you will see on your left "The Bush Inn". As the lane bends right you should leave it to continue straight on along a footpath, still marked as the Itchen Way, running parallel with the pub garden on your left. This leads you to the river Itchen which you should cross by way of a wooden bridge. This spot has to be one of my all time favourite places, its natural tranquility offering a real haven for wildlife. Look out for the many trout that enjoy the fast flow of the river as you cross the bridge.

After the bridge, turn left to follow a footpath which runs between the main river on your left and a smaller arm on the right. After some distance, follow the path as it turns right over the arm of the river by way of a footbridge. Here you will meet a lane which you should follow uphill, passing two thatched cottages on the left as you progress. You will soon arrive at a small green on the left, where you should turn left to go diagonally across the green and reach a road, the B3047. You are now at Itchen Stoke. Turn left along the road, taking great care as you go and pass a number of lovely cottages one of which used to be the old forge. After the cottage "Rivers Keep", turn left onto a track signposted as a footpath and also as part of the Itchen Way.

The track leads to a stile beside a farm gate which you should cross. Continue ahead for approximately twenty paces to meet and cross a second stile into a field. Go straight across the field where, if in doubt, you should follow the line of some telegraph poles and at the far side, go over a small brick bridge which crosses another arm of the Itchen. Thereafter, you should go diagonally left heading for another, this time wooden bridge, to cross a stile and then the bridge itself over the main part of the river. Watching the fast flowing crystal clear waters, you can see why Charles Kingsley chose this valley to write his charming tale "The Water Babies". After the bridge you should turn right and then almost immediately left ignoring a stile directly ahead. This soon leads you to another bridge over the river which you should cross to continue on a path still going straight on.

Ignore a footpath off to the right and continue ahead between banks which become steeper as you progress. This eventually leads out to a narrow lane which you should cross to continue your route ahead, again along a path between steep banks. This path is signposted as a bridleway and climbs gently uphill. Sometime later, you should ignore a footpath off to the left to continue ahead, where eventually you will enter Hampage Wood. In this wood once stood The Gospel Oak from where sermons were preached for the building of a church at Ovington.

The path, which can be extremely muddy in wet weather, winds through the wood to eventually reach a disused coppice. It then becomes wider and follows a field on your left and later suddenly leaves the wood to arrive at "Hampage Farm" and its huge farmhouse. There is a wide grass track running parallel with the path at this point, both of which lead out to a wide track, a bridleway **(OS. 545306).** Turn right here away from the farm, to follow the bridleway which runs through the centre of Hampage Wood. As you progress, you should ignore all turnings off and in particular, a wide grass crossing track to continue ahead. The track eventually bends round to the left and runs alongside Hampage Wood on your left with fields on the right. The woodland at this point is predominantly hazel and was obviously once a coppice.

As the woodland ends you will meet a gate through which you should pass to continue ahead along a hedged track between fields. This eventually leads out to the farm yard of

"Avington Manor Farm", where you should pass through a wooden gate on to a lane. Immediately after, you should turn left along the lane for approximately thirty paces, to then leave the lane passing through a farm gate ahead into a field. Follow the left hand perimeter of the field and at the far left hand corner, pass through another gate to re-enter Hampage Wood. You should now carry straight on along a wide track through the wood which is now markedly different to the woodland passed earlier, the trees being much older.

Ignore any crossing tracks or turnings off and continue ahead through the wood eventually passing through a unique stile, to once again meet and cross the A31. Join a tarmac drive the other side, marked "no cars - bridleway only" and follow this heading for a farm. There are excellent views all around now of the surrounding countryside. Just before the farm, you will meet a crossing track where you should turn left onto a signposted bridleway, part of the new extension to the South Downs Way. The track leads down into Temple Valley which sweeps majestically off to your right. At the bottom you should ignore a track off to the right to continue ahead, now uphill, to cross Ovington Down. Here there are more views to be enjoyed and on a clear day, Butser Hill is visible ahead in the distance.

The track descends to pass through a wooden gate and continues its undulating route to eventually meet a lane. As a guide, back to your right at this point is a lovely old flint barn in the centre of a field. Cross the lane and carry straight on along a wide track ahead, signposted as a bridleway and by way of a white acorn, as the South Downs Way. Pass through a wooden gate and follow the track up Gander Down to later meet a crossing track beside a barn on your right (OS. 555279). Here you should turn left to follow another track along the right hand perimeter of a field.

The track follows the field perimeter where just before the field ends, you should look out for a small wooden gate beside a larger metal farm gate on your right. Pass through the gate and go straight across the centre of a field, heading for the far top left hand corner. As you cross descending into the valley, you should ignore a track left which leads to Tichborne, its church being just visible from here. Continue your route to the bottom of the valley and up the other side, now following the left hand perimeter of the field. A small wooden gate in the field corner will soon come into view. On meeting the gate, it is worth pausing to catch your breath and look back across the valley to Gander Down where General Gander, another victim of the Battle of Cheriton, is said to be buried.

Pass through the gate and follow a narrow path ahead winding through deciduous woodland to meet and pass through another wooden gate sometime later. After the gate turn left going downhill along a narrow tarmac farm track, where after a short distance you should ignore a track off to the left beside a barn. You should also ignore another track off to the right shortly after. The farm track continues uphill and passes a tree lined hedge, after which the tarmac ends. Soon after, you will pass a track off to the right which you should ignore to continue your route ahead now going downhill.

The track leads out between a cluster of pretty cottages and houses known as "Hill Houses". Continue straight on ignoring turnings off to the left and right marked as a bridleway and footpath respectively. You will now follow a tarmac lane downhill, where after a short distance you will pass a cottage on your right aptly named "Thatched Cottage". Immediately after, take a footpath right and pass through a small wooden gate into a field. Go diagonally left across the centre of the field to the far corner, heading for the church tower in the distance.

At the far corner, cross over a stile to join a fenced path. On your right as a guide, is a small childrens playground and a cricket pitch. Here you should bear immediately left over another stile and go straight across a field heading for the church yard. On reaching the church yard, continue straight on following its perimeter until you meet a garden fence ahead. Here you should turn right to pass through a small gate into the church yard itself and continue ahead keeping to the left hand perimeter following its attractive flint wall. On meeting the main church path which is gravel, turn left through the ornate gates and follow the path between cottages to arrive at a road in the centre of Cheriton village. Cross the road and follow a gravel path across the centre of the village green to cross the river Itchen for the last time and reach the Post Office, our starting point.

ACCOMMODATION

The Flower Pots Inn, Cheriton. Tel: 0962 771318

Virtually on the walk, this is an ideal base from which to start and to explore the Itchen valley further. Accommodation is in some outbuildings, sensible if popular bars tend to keep you awake.

Woodcote Manor, Bramdean. Tel: 0962 771793

If you want to continue to surround yourself in history, then this is the place to stay. Three quarters of a mile from the walk, accommodation is in a beautiful 14th century manor house. One can even stay in the same room used by Mary Queen of Scotts before her wedding to Philip II of Spain.

Youth Hostel, Winchester YHA, Winchester. Tel: 0962 853723

Six miles from the walk, the youth hostel is set in an 18th century water mill on the river Itchen. Full of character, the youth hostel is an interesting place to stay but does get full with international visitors in summer.

Camping, River Park Leisure Centre, Winchester. Tel: 0962 869525

Six miles from the walk, this is a popular but pleasant site close to Winchester city centre. An ideal place to explore south east Hampshire.

THE MEAN MEON MEANDER

Distance: 15½ miles (24.25 km)

Time: Allow approximately 7 hours

Map: Ordnance Survey Landranger Maps 185 and 196

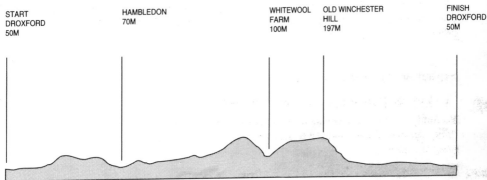

| START DROXFORD 50M | HAMBLEDON 70M | | WHITEWOOL FARM 100M | OLD WINCHESTER HILL 197M | FINISH DROXFORD 50M |

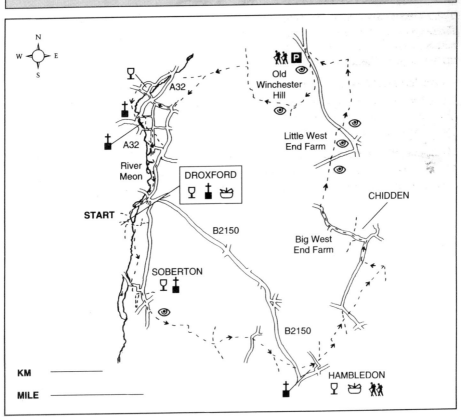

Walk Summary

The Mean Meon Meander is a walk with two very distinct halves. One half explores the gentle Meon valley, known locally as the Happy Valley, following the river Meon itself and passing through charming villages. The other half traverses the western tip of the South Downs with their grass slopes and magnificent views to the sea. The going is fairly easy though there is one very steep descent just before Old Winchester Hill, from where the walker is rewarded with some of the best views in Hampshire. The main danger, is that there are so many distractions that the walk can become longer than at first planned and care is needed if you are to finish the last stages before dark.

Start - OS. 606183 Map 185

The walk starts from Droxford which is easy to get to being situated on the A32 between Alton and Fareham. There is a rough square leading off to the church opposite Manor Cottages where you can park, though some spaces are reserved for local residents so please park considerately. There are two good alternative starting points, one is Hambledon village (OS. 646152 Map 196), which is ideal if you are starting early allowing you the choice of several good lunchtime pub stops. The second is Old Winchester Hill (OS. 647210 Map 185) which has a parking area. The nearest railway station is Fareham, seven miles south of Droxford. From here you can take a bus.

THE MEAN MEON MEANDER

Before setting off, it is worth finding out a little about the village from which we are starting.

Droxford (OS. 606183 Map 185). It is perhaps the inhabitants of Droxford rather than the buildings to whom we should first be introduced. Many of them are descendants of the Meonware, a Jutish tribe who settled here in early Saxon history. Apart from giving the river and the valley their names, they also baptised Droxford, Droxford being Saxon for "ford at the dry or shallow place". We can derive from this that Droxford was once an important river crossing when the waters were much deeper than they are today.

Much of the village today dates from the 17th and 18th centuries. It was in the 17th century that Izaak Walton, author of "The Complete Angler", married the rector's daughter, Anne Hawkins. He often stayed at the rectory and fished the river running conveniently close to the house. It is known that he held the river in high regard for he penned that it "exceeds all England for swift, shallow, clear, pleasant brooks and store of trout". You can still find trout in the village today, although it is perhaps easier to locate them at one of the two hostelries, The Bakers Arms, a free house or the excellent 17th century White Horse, also a free house. Should you require a packed lunch, there is also a general stores.

From the parking area pass through the metal gate into the church yard of St. Mary All Saints church. Follow the gravel path heading for the church ignoring the Wayfarers Walk sign on your left, to pass in front of the church. Although you have only just started, the church is well worth a visit.

St. Mary All Saints Church, Droxford (OS. 607183 Map 185). The earliest parts of this beautiful church date from the 12th century. The main item of interest is a stone figure of a lady found buried in a nearby meadow and now resting in the south chapel. She is believed (but not proven) to be the mother of John de Drokensford, son of a local squire in the 14th century, later to become the Bishop of Bath and Wells. The figure had probably been removed from the church to avoid destruction during the Civil War.

Before leaving, look out for a hangman's noose which is said to appear hanging from the church ceiling, though no reason can be found for this ghostly apparition.

From the church entrance leave the church yard via an exit in the wall. Immediately after, turn left to follow a path along the church yard perimeter, where as you continue the path gradually widens into a track. At this point, at the end of the church yard on your left, you are now following the Wayfarers Walk marked by a black arrow on a white background. Stay on the track to meet and cross the river Meon. This is a lovely place to rest awhile or perhaps to return to at the end of your walk.

Continue ahead along the left hand perimeter of a field crossing a muddy area via a second bridge, immediately after which you should turn right over a stile into another field. Follow the right hand perimeter of the field and at the far side cross another stile into a third field. Here the river Meon momentarily rejoins your route. Follow the right hand perimeter of the field and at the far side go over another stile to then go diagonally left, in the direction of the black arrows, across the next field. Head for a group of horse chestnut trees and then follow the path which runs along the right hand perimeter of the trees, where you should meet and cross another stile and continue straight on. The tree lined bank on your left is the old Meon Valley railway line. This part of the line has a place in modern history, as it was in a railway carriage near here that Winston Churchill, the War Cabinet and the Allied Chiefs made their final preparations for the invasion of Europe.

With war being thankfully impossible to imagine in this valley, continue straight on to eventually meet a stile over which you should pass to join a lane beside a small red brick bridge. Turn left to go up the lane passing over the old railway line, immediately after which you should turn right to join a narrow footpath. Do not be tempted here to turn right again onto the railway line, but turn left over a stile into a field. Go diagonally right across the field to meet the perimeter of the grave yard to Soberton church. As you cross the field, the large building on your left is appropriately called "The Towers".

Do not be tempted to continue further across the field, but follow the perimeter of the graveyard round to exit the field via a stile beside a wooden farm gate. This is adjacent to the entrance to the church. Welcome to the village of Soberton.

Soberton (OS. 611167 Map 185) is set on a rise above the river Meon, its unusual church tower dominating the sky line. The tower, a credit to any ghost film, is guarded by grinning stone demons and frowning gargoyles. Most unusual of all, in the tower's west face, is the carving of a skull set between two heads, those of a man and a woman. By the head of the man is a key and the woman a pail. Legend has it that the tower was built from monies donated by two servants, a butler and a milkmade, though what connection the skull has is unknown. In keeping with the legend, the tower was restored in 1880 by subscriptions from servants all over Hampshire.

Outside the church is a stone coffin, believed to be Roman. The village itself is a scattering of unspoilt cottages, the centre (if it has one) being the green between the church and The White Lion pub, Whitbread, a pleasant if early stop for some refreshments. The White Lion also has a restaurant.

After the stile turn right along a tarmac drive leading away from the church into the village of Soberton. This leads to a lane in front of "The White Lion" pub. Turn right along the lane and go downhill passing many charming cottages, to reach a crossroads just after the village hall on your left. Go over the crossroads and continue ahead along a lane opposite signposted to Hoe Cross, Hambledon and Denmead. This takes you gently uphill and just after the lane bends right, you will pass the entrance to "Westdown Cottage". Here you should leave the lane turning left on to a track signposted as a footpath and also part of the Wayfarers Walk.

The track, also a driveway, goes uphill passing to the right of "Westdown Cottage". At the end of the drive, you will meet another house, "Birds Eye View", where the drive bends right away from the property. Here you should leave the drive and turn left to go uphill beside a garage to reach and cross a stile into a field. Follow the left hand perimeter of the field, still going uphill, which in summer is a brightly coloured blanket of wild flowers. As you climb, it is worth pausing awhile to look back over the village of Soberton and a large house in the distance to the far side of the Meon valley, "Middlington House". Go over a stile and continue ahead to reach and cross another stile into the next field.

Go straight on across the centre of the field, where you will gain panoramic views. To the north, Old Winchester Hill and Wether Down with its aerial masts. To the left of Old Winchester Hill at the other side of the Meon valley, you can also see Beacon Hill and its coombe. To the south on a clear day the Isle of Wight and the numerous chimneys of Fawley oil refinery are visible. Cross over another stile and go across the centre of the next field bearing slightly left and at the far side cross two more stiles into another field. Once again, you should continue straight on to reach the far side where you should turn right and follow a track, keeping to the left hand perimeter of the field.

After approximately one hundred metres turn left, thereby leaving the track, in the direction of the black arrows to follow a narrow path through a strip of woodland. Take care not to miss this. The path continues for approximately a third of a mile to eventually meet a stile. Go over the stile and continue ahead along a wide track which after a short distance bends left. Here you should leave the track turning right along another track, still signposted as the Wayfarers Walk. This leads to a field with a gate where you should turn left over a stile beside the gate and follow the left hand perimeter of the field with views to your right across to Portsdown Hill. It is hard to believe from here, that at the other side of Portsdown Hill is the sprawling city of Portsmouth. If you have good eyesight or binoculars, you can just distinguish ridges at regular intervals along the length of the hill. These are forts which were built to defend Portsmouth from an inland attack. As you can see, they are cunningly disguised. As it turned out, the forts were never needed and they became known as Palmerston's Folly, Palmerston being the Prime Minister who ordered their construction.

On joining another field, bear right to follow a track across the centre. As you continue, you will probably enjoy the best views throughout the walk of the Isle of Wight. At the far side, go over a stile beside a large metal gate and cross a lane ahead to follow a signposted footpath across the centre of another field. As a guide, the property on your left at this point is "East Hoe Manor". At the other side of the field, cross over a stile and turn right to follow the right hand perimeter of a field, running between a shallow bank on your left, probably an old field boundary and a fenced field on your right. You will soon meet a signposted footpath off to the right which you should ignore to bear slightly left and go across the corner of the field heading for a stile at the far side.

Go over the stile and carry straight on, ignoring a path off to the right. The path is now quite narrow and runs through woodland, predominantly deciduous. It soon joins a wide track where you should continue straight on through woodland along the top of a hill, until you meet a fork. Take the left hand fork to immediately reach and cross a stile and continue ahead, now going downhill, along a narrow fenced path still following the Wayfarers Walk. The path, which can be very slippery in wet weather, eventually leads out in front of a garden where you should turn left to continue down to a main road, the B2150.

Turn right along the road for approximately thirty paces and then left onto a footpath, still marked as part of the Wayfarers Walk. Pass to the right of the Police Station and carry straight on along the left of Stewarts Green. At the far side of the green, cross the road and continue along a fenced footpath running between houses to reach a field. Go across the field heading for Hambledon church ahead. At the far side of the field, pass through a kissing gate and continue ahead following a flint garden wall which encloses the old rectory. The path leads out to Hambledon church yard. If you wish to visit Hambledon and its church, turn right here.

Hambledon (OS. 646151 Map 196). *You arrive at Hambledon passing the church of St. Peter and St. Paul, the size of the church being an immediate clue to the village's past prosperity. The first church on this site was Saxon, the church today is mainly Norman with some substantial additions from the 13th and 19th centuries. Note the flags hanging in the church, these are the colours of the Hambledon Volunteers, formed to repel Napoleon's invasion that never came. Apart from the magnificent Norman arches, you may notice a piscina built in an odd position up high on one of the walls. Beside it sits a ledge, a small window and a narrow archway. This was once a hermit's cell. The hermit would be locked up here (supposedly willingly) to dedicate his life to God.*

From the church, you arrive at the square which leads out onto the High Street. The layout you may notice, with the square off to one side of the street leading to the church, is almost identical to Droxford as it is in many of the villages in this part of Hampshire. The village itself is built at a junction of three valleys. The site was immediately attractive to the Romans who built the first dwelling of any size here. After the Romans, came the Saxons who called the village Hamelanduna. By the time of The Domesday book, the name had changed to Ambledune and then recorded in a Parliamentary survey in 1647, as Hambledon.

The first step to the village's prosperity came when Henry III granted the Bishop of Winchester the right of a weekly market at Hambledon. The village continued to grow in propserity despite the black death and the unsettled politics of the time and in 1612, received another boost when James I granted Hambledon the right to hold two fairs a year. It was probably the fairs that gave the name to nearby Broad Halfpenny Down as a broad halfpenny was the standard toll paid to enter a fair.

There were divided loyalties during the Civil War. Hambledon is famous for its Hambledon Boys who fought under Colonel Norton on the side of the Roundheads. They played a major part in the defeat of the Royalists at the Battle of Cheriton (see The Roundhead Round). On the Royalists side, Hambledon hid the King on his escape to France. He stayed as a guest of Colonel Gounter of "Bury Lodge" at the cottage of his brother-in-law, Thomas Symonds. The cottage is now known as "King's Nest". A tribute to Symonds is to be found in the form of a tall stone at the base of the church tower.

At the beginning of the 19th century, Hambledon sadly fell into decline, the market dwindled and the market covering, through neglect, one day collapsed. The writer, Cobbett, whilst riding this way in 1826 recorded Hambledon as being a "tumbledown rubbishy place". Today, Hambledon prospers again, the village has two successful industries, mineral water (ale was once also brewed here, until a careless German dropped a bomb on the place) and wine, for Hambledon has a vineyard. Both the water and the wine can be purchased from the village stores and I can personally recommend both. There are two good hostelries close to the church, The New Inn an 18th century coaching inn and The George Inn, a free house. Both serve food.

Return to our route via the church yard, commonly grazed by sheep in the traditional fashion.

Continue straight on through the church yard, thereby leaving the Wayfarers Walk, passing to the left of the church to meet and cross a lane. Join a footpath ahead and pass to the right of Hambledon County First School, after which you should ignore a footpath off to the left which leads over Windmill Down. Continue straight on along a narrow fenced path which leads to a tarmac drive. Cross the drive and continue ahead to pass through one of the reasons for Hambledon's fame, its vineyard.

On reaching a track, turn left to go uphill along the track which ends after a short distance beside two gates. Here you should join a narrow sometimes overgrown footpath and continue ahead with the vineyard on your left and a hedgerow on the right. The footpath soon bears right over a stile into a field. Go across the field heading for some trees the other side, where the grand house just below on your right is "Park House". *i* This is an Elizabethan house and has a priest hole, indicating another role in Hambledon's history.

At the far side of the field go over a stile and pass through a narrow strip of woodland, to join another field where you should turn left and follow the left hand perimeter. As the perimeter bears left however, you should continue straight on across the centre of the field and head for the wooden building in the distance ahead, the now re-sited Hambledon Cricket Club. At the end of the field, cross over a stile and then cross a road ahead to enter Ridge Meadow, Home of Hambledon Cricket Club.

i **Hambledon Cricket Club (OS. 653163 Map 185).** *Perhaps Hambledon's greatest claim to fame is not its role in the Civil War, but as the birth place of English cricket. Although cricket had been played in various forms all over England, it was at Hambledon that the first rules of the modern game were laid down and adhered to. The original team played on Broad Halfpenny Down, now remembered by a stone memorial and The Bat and Ball Inn. The club later moved to its present site in 1782.*

Hambledon's greatest success came in the 18th century. In 1772 they beat England by fiftythree runs and in 1774 England again, this time by an innings and fiftytwo runs. Finally in 1777, they had their greatest victory when they conquered England by an innings and one hundred and sixtyeight runs. Ironically during this period, the game of cricket was technically illegal, banned by Henry VIII to try and preserve the more essential practice of archery.

The club attracted many gentlemen and celebrities to its game in its heyday. The rapid decline of the club came with the war with France during the late 18th century, when many of the gentlemen left to fight. The first nail in the coffin came with the setting up of

Mary-Le-Bone Cricket Club (MCC) in London by the then president of the Hambledon club. The last entry in the original club's minutes book is dated 21st September, 1796 and simply but sadly reads, "No gentlemen".

Although no-where near as glorious, the club still continues to this day. If you are lucky enough you may catch a game whilst passing and it is worth stopping if only to pay tribute to the founders of the now international gentlemens game.

Follow the right hand perimter of the cricket pitch and at the far side, carry straight on along a fenced path which leads into a field. Here you should continue ahead along a path between two fields and when you meet a hedgerow, carry straight on keeping the hedgerow to your right, now following the right hand perimeter of the field. Continue to follow the field perimeter round until you see a gap in the hedge on your right. Pass through the gap and go over a stile into the next field, which you should cross by way of a well defined path. This is an extremely large field and the crossing seems to take an age. On nearing the other side, the farm in view ahead is "Hermitage Farm". At the other side of the field, turn left to follow the right hand perimeter.

As you continue, there are good views to your right of the hamlet of Chidden and to the left of Hambledon cricket pitch. You will eventually meet a narrow lane on to which you should turn right and follow to Chidden. When you reach a "T" junction beside "Chidden Farm", turn left to follow another lane signposted to Meonstoke and Droxford. Stay on the lane which climbs uphill to pass farm buildings and immediately after "2 and 1 Cottages", follow it downhill again. At the base of the hill ignore a lane off to the left signposted to Hambledon, the farm in the distance on your left here is "Big West End Farm".

Continue on the lane which climbs again to the top of a hill, where the lane bends right and soon after, left. You should leave the lane at this point and turn right on to a gravel track **(OS. 648184 Map 185)**. The track climbs steadily uphill where, as you continue, you will enjoy fantastic views behind over the Isle of Wight. After approximately half a mile, the track meets a lane in front of "Little West End Farm", which you should cross. You should then pass through a farm gate into "Little West End Farm" and continue straight through the farm yard to leave it via two farm gates into a field. Go straight on along the right hand perimeter of the field with fantastic views left over almost the entire walk and in particular, the Meon valley. Ahead of you now, is Old Winchester Hill fort and ahead to the left, Beacon Hill.

At the far side of the field, cross over a stile into the next field and continue along the right hand perimeter to reach and pass through a metal gate on to a lane. Cross the lane, pass over a stile and go straight across a field now going gently downhill (if the way is unclear follow the line of the telegraph poles). Here again you have excellent views, although this time to the north where straight ahead of you slightly to the right, is East Meon church with its tiled spire. East Meon incidentally, is the source of the river Meon. Further to your right, the aerial masts of Wether Down are much closer now. At the other side of the field, cross over a stile and go across a very narrow field to meet and cross another stile. Here you should go down a very steep hill, taking great care as you go and again you should follow in the general direction of the telegraph poles to meet a small wooden gate in the far left hand corner.

Pass through the gate and continue straight ahead along the left hand perimeter of the next field heading for some houses. Leave the field beside the houses via a metal farm gate and carry straight on to meet a wide gravel track. Do not turn right but maintain your course between fields heading for "White Wood Farm". On reaching the farm, the track becomes concrete. Continue straight on through the farm yard with the thatched farm house ahead and at the far side, turn left in front of a gate. Ignore a turning right soon after, and carry straight on along a concrete track heading for Old Winchester Hill. You are now following the new extension to the South Downs Way.

After a short distance, pass through a metal gate where the concrete track ends. Continue straight ahead along a fenced track between fields going gently uphill. The track leads up to a set of four gates in front of a disused chalk quarry, where you should pass through the second gate on your right (in other words the third on your left!) which is marked by a blue arrow as a bridleway. This leads diagonally up the side of Old Winchester Hill with lovely views as you near the top over the valley below and Butser Hill in the distance.

At the top of the hill the track meets a farm gate through which you should pass to reach a lane. Turn left along the lane taking care as you go as regards traffic - this is a popular haunt for day trippers. Continue until you reach the first parking area on your right. Turn right at this point passing an Old Winchester Hill National Nature Reserve Information sign, to lead out on to the hill where you will enjoy superb views south over the Meon valley.

On reaching a junction of paths, turn left to follow a well trodden grass path following the side of the hill which later bends very gently right. Do not be tempted to go downhill but stay along the top of the hill, where to your right now is Old Winchester Hill fort itself. Follow the path to eventually meet a gravel track on to which you should turn right, passing another National Nature Reserve sign for Old Winchester Hill **(OS. 647208 Map 185).** Continue straight on with woodland on your right and open fields to the left. You should ignore two tracks, one soon after the other, off to the right and stay on the track to eventually meet a wooden kissing gate. Pass through the gate to arrive at Old Winchester Hill fort.

The track bends left and then right to pass between the ramparts of the hill fort itself and passes a dew pond on the right. Continue across the centre of the fort along a grass track, which in summer is a mass of chalkland flowers. At the centre of the hill fort there is a trig point and direction finder confirming that the fort is 648 ft above sea level. Here you can enjoy excellent panoramic views.

Old Winchester Hill and Hill Fort, 648ft/197m (OS. 642205 Map 185). You can immediately see why the fort's iron age builders chose this position. Set on a steep sided spur, the fort commands views over most of Hampshire and on a clear day, even some parts of Wiltshire. Legend has it that the fort was the original site of the great city of Winchester, hence the name Old Winchester. At the time of the fort's existence, Winchester would have been nothing more than a Roman station. With the coming of the Saxons, many of the hill forts were abandoned and it could well be that the inhabitants of this fort resettled at the Winchester of today. Also within the hill fort are several round barrows, some with concave tops indicating that they have been robbed.

In 1954, the Nature Conservancy Council acquired the site and now protect its unique collection of chalkland flowers and insects.

After the trig point, continue straight on to go gently downhill. At the other side of the hill fort bear left to take a narrow path downhill to the left of the ramparts, following a fence on your left. Leave the hill fort via a stile and continue steeply downhill through yew trees taking heed of the signs not to wander off the path, as the adjacent areas may still have remains of unexploded shells. Continue to eventually meet and pass through a small gate and follow a fenced path between fields going gently downhill, with views to your right of the Meon valley.

At the corner of the field on your right, the path bends right continuing between fields and soon after, left. Shortly after this, the path bends right again, at which point you should leave it taking a somewhat hidden footpath on your left through a narrow strip of woodland. This is marked by a yellow circle painted on a tree as you enter the woodland (OS. 634208 Map 185). The path winds through the wood to eventually lead out to a farm track onto which you should turn right. This runs between fields and graduates into a concrete track, shortly after which you should take the first track off to the left, this time marked by a yellow arrow.

This track also runs between fields and later narrows to become a path often sharing its route with a stream in wet weather. As a result of this, there is a smaller path running parallel just above the stream on the right hand bank. This follows the stream and crosses it at points where you will find stepping stones have been provided. The path continues for approximately half a mile until it meets a red brick bridge ahead. This is in fact part of the now disused Meon Valley railway line. Just before the bridge, you should pass between some wooden rails and then go up some steps to join the railway line itself. Turn left to follow the line. This is a pleasant walk with the odd bench conveniently sited to rest the weary walker.

After approximately two thirds of a mile the path suddenly descends to the left of the railway embankment to meet a lane. At this point you can see the reason for leaving the line, that a bridge no longer exists to continue the route. Turn right along the lane, thereby leaving the railway line and ignore another lane off to the right almost immediately after, to continue bearing left as you go. Stay on the lane to pass a cottage "Long View" and after a short distance, ignore another lane off to the left between houses, "The Limes" and "Prospect Cottage" and carry straight on to meet the main road, the A32.

Cross the main road with care and continue straight ahead along a lane signposted as the start of Exton village. Soon after, you will cross a pretty brick bridge over the river Meon leading into Exton itself, where to your right you will find "The Shoe" pub, a free house which serves food. The bar is decorated with old shoes and the pub garden overlooks the river - a lovely place to stop and rest your tired limbs!

Our route however, is left just before the pub along a lane following a flint wall on your right. To the left, the lane is lined by picturesque cottages, one in particular with a low thatched roof. Continue your route and follow the lane as it bends left, ignoring two turnings off to the right. You will now find a flint wall on your left and open fields to the right. As the lane bends round to the right, you should leave it to continue straight on along a grass footpath between an old barn and a wooden fence. Shortly after, pass through a wooden kissing gate and bear slightly left to follow the right hand perimeter of an open field. After a short distance, leave the field perimeter to continue straight on across the field to pass through a gap in the wooden fence. The river Meon follows your route to your left at this point.

Leave the field via a wooden stile to arrive at a small green between cottages with Corhampton church ahead of you. Continue ahead and then turn left along a drive to reach the main road, the A32, once more. If you wish to visit the church, turn right along the road to reach the entrance.

Corhampton Church (Os. 610203 Map 185). *This little church just oozing with character, is unusual in that it has no dedication and has remained almost unaltered from when it was built approximately one thousand years ago. It is also unusual in that it was built on an artifical mound. The early Christians shied away from such mounds believing them to be guarded by evil spirits of the pagan religions.*

The church has several interesting features. Just east of the south porch is a sundial divided into eight sections. This is because the Saxons divided their day by eight and not twelve. The sundial is one of the earliest surviving in the county. Inside there are several well preserved wall paintings, believed to date from the 12th century.

The church yard is dominated by a huge yew which is over a thousand years old and probably planted at the time the church was built. The early Christians planted yews in church yards to placate the local population who still held on to their pagan beliefs. The yew tree for them was sacred as they believed it warded off evil spirits. The early Christians also allowed the local population to hold their pagan festivities in the church yard. In 1285 the Statutes of Winchester forbade this practice, though right up to the 16th century, many villages still held the May dance in church yards.

As you leave the church yard you will notice a stone coffin now used as a flower bed. This is Roman, the body it contained is now buried in Meonstoke church yard.

To continue our route, turn left for a short distance along the A32 passing "Corhampton Mill" on your left. On the right hand side of the road, look out for an old milestone stating that London is 62 miles and Gosport 15 miles. Continue for a short distance until you meet a road turning off to the right beside the Post Office and General Stores. Cross the main road to take the road past the Post Office and continue passing St. Andrew's Green on your left.

After the last bungalow on your right, take a tarmac footpath right which soon leads into the church yard of St. Andrews at Meonstoke.

St. Andrews, Meonstoke (OS. 612203 Map 185). *This church must be set in one of the most beautiful locations in Hampshire. Surrounded by a large church yard, the church looks out over a beautiful garden which leads down to the sparkling waters of the river Meon. The church itself is 13th century and must have been quite a feat of engineering in its day, being built on what would have been then, nothing but marshland.*

Sadly, this picturesque church remembers amongst its dead twentytwo men from the village who were killed in the First World War, a devastating loss for a village of such a small size.

Continue through the church yard and leave it to turn left on to a lane beside a well kept garden. The lane leads out to "The Bucks Head", Pheonix Breweries, a pub with a varied menu and small beer garden. Turn left onto the lane beside the pub and continue uphill staying on the lane as it bends right beside a small green with a seat. You will now pass through the centre of Meonstoke, a cluster of lovely period houses and cottages.

As the lane eventually bears left, you should leave it to continue ahead along a much narrower lane signposted to Meonstoke Infant School. Pass to the right of the school and carry straight on as the lane ends to follow a fenced footpath between fields. The fences soon disappear and the path, now grass, continues between an avenue of trees. You should ignore all turnings off to eventually meet a stile beside a gate. Go over the stile on to a lane and turn right passing the entrance to "Meonstoke House". Continue until you reach a wide gravel drive on your right signposted as a footpath and to "Longmeadow House" which you should take.

After approximately thirty paces leave the track as it bends right, to carry straight on along a narrow footpath through scrubland. This footpath continues for some distance, passing through woodland which has in appearance by the many rotting tree stumps, survived some violent storms. At one point it crosses a gravel track and continues ahead, re-entering the woodland. The path eventually leads out onto a tarmac drive beside a house, which you should follow straight on to meet a road, the B2150.

Cross the road and turn left for approximately forty metres taking care as you go, to meet a small group of cottages. Take the first turning right which is a narrow lane signposted as a dead end. This leads down past fields to a small bridge where you cross the river Meon once more. The crossing here is said to be haunted by a coach and horses. The story goes, that a coach overturned at this point drowning its passengers (remember the waters were much deeper then). The coach is said to reappear on the anniversary of the accident. Hopefully, you will walk this way on a different day!

Follow a tarmac path the other side which leads you to the picturesque "Droxford Mill" where another small bridge takes you over the mill race. The mill was built in 1740 and operated until 1905 when it closed. The house was restored in 1953 and is now a private residence. The path then leads out to a narrow lane which you should follow for approximately twenty paces before turning left over a stile into a field.

Follow the right hand perimeter of the field for a short distance and take the first turning right through a kissing gate to enter St. Mary All Saints church yard at Droxford. Do not turn left along the path which as a point of note, is made up of old headstones. Our route is straight ahead along the right hand side of the church yard to exit via a metal gate thereby arriving at the car park, our starting point.

ACCOMMODATION

The White Horse, Droxford. Tel: 0489 877490

Fifty metres from the walk, this is a 17th century coaching inn which has retained its character. The rooms are tastefully furnished and you do not have to leave the inn to enjoy a good meal, complimented by well chosen ale.

Moortown Farmhouse, Soberton. Tel: 0489 877256

Two hundred metres from the walk, this is an eight acre horse farm set close to the village centre and therefore the pub! The rooms are comfortable and the hosts very friendly.

Youth Hostel, Winchester YHA, Winchester. Tel: 0962 853723

Twelve miles from the walk, the youth hostel is set in an 18th century water mill on the river Itchen. Full of character, the youth hostel is an interesting place to stay, but does get full with international visitors in summer.

Camping, Riverpark Leisure Centre, Winchester. Tel: 0962 869525

Twelve miles from the walk, this is a popular but pleasant site close to Winchester city centre.

SOME
FURTHER
ADVENTURES

Coming soon

"10 Adventurous Walks in Berkshire"